four FOR THE Road

OTHER BOOKS BY THIS AUTHOR

The Leap Year (2017)

*Does a family who travel together, stay together?
One mother finds out...*

JANE DELAHAY

Providing professional book design and printing services
for indie authors to tell their stories and follow their dreams

www.accentia.com.au

First published 2018

Publishing Partner: Accentia Design Pty Ltd
Cover image: © 2018 by Anna Blatman (www.annablatman.com)
Cover design: Michelle Hessing
Copy editing: Heather Bryant

Copyright © Jane Delahay, 2018

The moral right of the author has been asserted.

All rights reserved.

Without limiting the rights under copyright restricted above, no part of this publication may be reproduced, in any form or by any means (electronic, mechanical, photocopying, recording or otherwise), without the prior written permission of both the copyright owner and the above publishing partner of this book.

Typesetting & Prepared for Publication by: Accentia Design

A Cataloguing-in-Publication record is available from the National Library of Australia.

ISBN: 978-0-6482776-3-7 (Paperback)
ISBN: 978-0-6482776-4-4 (ePub)

For Imogen & Trinity

PROLOGUE

Four for the Road

In 1998 my husband I travelled to Northern England and Scotland with his sister. It was a trip I remembered fondly, in fact, it was one of my favourite trips I had ever been on. The magnificence of the Scottish Highlands, the elegance and history of Edinburgh, and the foot loose and fancy free drive through the countryside in our red Audi... they were such marvellous memories. We were mesmerised at the beauty of this rugged landscape, it was breathtakingly picturesque, straight from a chocolate box. Coming from a sunburnt country like Australia, it was a whole new world, a world I immediately fell in love with.

My husband and I had taken a leap of faith back in the 1990's, uprooted and left Australia to live and work in the United Kingdom. We had planned to be there for a year, but we returned home four years later with a baby girl in tow. This trip is etched in my memory, I spoke about it often, and wanted to re-create it with our teenage children. It had been a desire for me to show our children this magnificent country and take them on a driving tour of England and Scotland. Nineteen years later, and my dream came true—we were on our way to re-create the trip of my memories.

The idea to take the children on a driving holiday has always been a question of when. Their teenage years seemed most appropriate – at least by then they could carry their own bags—so we decided on thirteen and sixteen.

A lot had changed in nineteen years, and the whimsical holiday we had back in the nineties was to pale into insignificance of travelling in 2017. We are a family of travellers. My children are used to packing a suitcase and heading for distant countries or neighbouring islands. I have always thought I had the 'wanderlust gene' and I hope I passed it on to my children.

I love travelling, it is all I have ever wanted to do. I spend my savings on it, I dream about it, I plan it. This obsession is greeted by my family with varying degrees of interest. My announcement of travelling to Los Angeles and New York a few years back was met with eagerness and anticipation – the news we were driving around England and Scotland in a few months' time was met with a slightly less degree of enthusiasm. "You'll see," I said. "It will be an adventure". By the looks on their faces, I might have well said, "We are going to trek the Amazon for our holiday." I was determined to make this the family holiday of a lifetime, I just wasn't sure how.

"You cannot discover anything in life without first getting lost"
– Jane Delahay

CHAPTER 1 – SANDGATE

The day we landed in England was overshadowed by the fact my husband had to be taken off the aircraft by two paramedics. Not the best start to our holiday. A dodgy chocolate mousse the day before had given him salmonella poisoning and he became unconscious ten minutes into the flight. Whilst this was terribly frightening at the time, Raymond came around, and the staff on the plane were amazingly efficient at dealing with a passenger who had slumped in his seat, eyes rolling back into his head. I will be forever grateful that we miraculously happened to be on the same flight as a nurse and a paramedic. I told him that if he ever had to do that again, please don't do it at 30,000 feet.

The children were understandingly upset by the time we arrived on English soil. Our dearest friend, Jules came to pick us up at the airport and when just myself and the girls walked through the immigration doors, bleary eyed and shaken up, she excitedly looked around for the fourth member of our family. With an infectious laugh and a childlike zest for life, Jules was exuberant in her hugs and very excited to see us.

I however, was in need of a stiff drink. Before I could tell her where Raymond was, he was rolled out of the swinging doors in a wheelchair by an airport employee in a high vis vest.

Jules started laughing hysterically. "What in the hell happened to you?" After much laughter—and staring by other people waiting for their own friends and family at the arrival gates—we were in the car and on our way to Sandgate. The one bonus of my husband being in a wheelchair was getting through immigration in a flash. It had never happened to us before. On many occasions we had stood waiting haplessly in a snaking line for hours at immigration.

I was so happy to be back in the UK, I had missed the old girl. My ancestry is English, and I feel quite the deep rooted belonging to this most perfect island.

Whenever I land on English soil, I feel at home. It is a hard feeling to explain, but I sense I fit right into the Englishness of it all.

The eccentricities, the castles, and stately homes, the quaint stone villages, the architecture, the weather, the rituals, and the awe-inspiring landscapes … (I could go on!)

There are so many magical corners of this country ; it takes you by surprise and leaves you standing there with your mouth wide open in wonder. I do love my sunburnt country too, it is my home, but I feel a certain infinity with the mother country.

We met Jules and Kate twenty years ago in a small pub in Lambeth in South London when we were the new Aussie kids on the block. Raymond and Kate worked together, they became firm friends instantly. The fact that Jules and I hit it off too was a windfall in the friendship stakes.

My eldest daughter, Aurora is thoughtful and introspective with a warm and generous spirit. Quiet in nature, she rarely sparks up conversations; her introverted personality would rather scan her surroundings for understanding than talk about them. Her 'go with the flow' disposition is a godsend on a family holiday. Adaptable and compliant, it is rare for her to be troubled by any travel situation, good or bad.

My youngest daughter, Coco is the exact opposite. She is outgoing, social with a terrific sense of humour. Everything in her world is awesome; she is the 'glass half-full' child. Confident and creative, she will never bore you with her stories; she is the fancy pants of the family. She is also the worst traveller.

I could not have had two more different children to share this adventure with.

Jules and Kate own a gorgeous seaside home overlooking the English Channel. While it is not the Great Barrier Reef, it is charming and quintessentially British. The indigo coloured sea is flat with a beach full of golf sized white pebbles. Interestingly the coastal village is called Sandgate but there is no sand on the beach. These pebbles are hard to navigate if you want to dip you toes in the water, scrunching underneath your feet and making your stride wobbly, more reminiscent of a night out on the tiles than a seaside walk.

Sandgate is a charming village located in the Shepway district of Kent. It stands on the coast at the foot of imposing and picturesque hills, with a view across to the French Coast. It has a fascinating history (like many villages in England). Sandgate was founded in 1773 by a ship builder and inevitably became a place where ship building prospered because of the close proximity to the sea. It is not a big village, but on our first night in England we were off to enjoy fish and chips on the beach for dinner. My husband crawled into bed to recover from the flight ordeal, and the rest of us took the opportunity to soak up an English summer at twilight.

I had almost forgotten about this most wonderful natural phenomenon, where England does not get dark until late at night. The days are long and perfect, with the sun rising at 6am and not disappearing under the sea until 10:30pm. As tourists, so many daylight hours was fabulous.

The night was still and mild, the sky was dark blue, and seagulls floated by riding the airwaves. Our fish and chips were enclosed in the obligatory newspaper, and we carried them to the shoreline to partake in a very English tradition. While my children are a fan of fish and chips, we rarely eat them at home. Not just because they are full of cholesterol, but in our busy lives there never seems to be time to chill out and have takeaway, even on Friday nights. The children were either off with their friends, or choose more sophisticated takeaway options, like Malaysian. But we were on holidays, so a bit of junk food was going to be the norm anyway—might as well start then.

Traversing those white pebbles on the beach was a struggle with armfuls of food, Jules had ordered enough to feed an army. Those gliding seagulls were in for a treat. We finally found a suitable place to park ourselves and sat down. I had to make a mould out of the beach pebbles so my butt could sit comfortably while I ate.

Pebbles have this very strange sound when you knock them together, like an egg cracking.

As I shifted myself in the pebbles to get comfortable my bum sounded like I was letting off farts. I realised Aurora and Coco were trying to do the same, making their own farting noises. We were like a chorus of people who sounded like they had been eating lentils all day. It wasn't terribly comfortable, but the company was beautiful and I was happy to see our friends after a hiatus of two years.

The next morning we headed into another port town on the English Channel, Folkestone to do some touristy stuff while I collected Raymond's medication for his sky-high health dramas. The salmonella was not something he wanted lingering for the duration of the holiday. The local clinic was fantastic and armed us with several bottles of pills and potions.

Folkestone is another seaport town in the Shepway district. It has a very pleasing harbour that once had a thriving ferry service but now has a newly installed 'Harbour Arm' ,it's a great place to stroll along or sip champagne at the lighthouse bar, which is exactly what we did.

Jules and Kate had morning errands to run and we were happy to mooch about and stroll the old streets of this handsome town. There is a very quaint street here called the 'Old High Street', all cobblestoned and almost a vertical walk down to the harbour. But it is worth meandering along to look inside the windows of the dear little shops that line the edges. The shop fronts are all painted in vibrant colours, the hues of pink, orange and green make it look quite tropical, like a pina colada. It was a sunny morning and the colours bounced off the sky and gave it quite the festive feel.

We found a delightful little cake shop with the most enormous Victoria sponge in the window (my favourite cake). I hadn't had a piece that size in years, and it was delicious.

Folkestone is a lovely town to just wander, especially in the older parts. The Parish Church of St Mary and St Eanswythe is a hidden gem, and the gardens surrounding it are rich and well kept. It is one of the nicest churches I have seen. The exterior has this dark grey stone facade with a haphazard graveyard that would probably look right at home in a spooky movie, but is actually quite tranquil. The church dates back to 670AD. There are little signs dotted along the pavements to tell you a bit about the history and it made for interesting reading.

I put my travel guide hat on and explained to the girls that generations of families had been baptised, married and farewelled in this church, their blank faces gave me all the information I needed, they were bored.

There are two words that parents of teenagers will hear every day: Wi-Fi. In 1998 this word didn't exist, well not in the same sense that is does now. These four letters are a teenager's lifeline. I don't even pretend to understand the machinations of all of those social media sites—I truly struggle just to understand why my children's phones have to be with them every minute of the day. I never want to say, "in my day", as I usually get the eye rolling response, but really, in my day we didn't have anything we were that attached to—not even my Wham! records. I get it... it is 2017 and this is the way teenagers communicate.

I had taken them both out of school to traipse the English and Scottish countryside and they wanted to keep in touch with their friends. Albeit, the time zone would pose a problem that they didn't realise yet. FOMO (fear of missing out) was a distinct possibility. Raymond and I had to work out what screen time was actually acceptable during our holidays; too many times we were met with the distracted teenage eye looking up over the screen. I'm sure half the time they didn't actually know what I said to them.

We couldn't ban their electronics altogether, that would have caused a mutiny, but we came to an agreement about the device time. They needed the down time, just like I did during "Aperitivo hour", but exactly what that would be was still to be decided. Jules said to me twenty four hours after we arrived that she was amazed that Aurora and Coco hadn't asked for the Wi-Fi password, little did they know I told them they were not to ask our hosts for the password as soon as they walked in the door. The time that lapsed was up to them, but I too was impressed they had waited at least twenty-four hours. They were itching to get back to the hi-tech world of 2017, the history lesson was over.

We had a few days to relax with our friends before we took off on our driving holiday and left it to them to decide on our itineraries. We hadn't visited many of the neighbouring towns before and were keen to get out and explore. It was decided we would visit Dungeness on the coast of Kent, it sounded intriguing, almost a bit magical, but I can assure you it is not. It is called the "Desert of England", and I could see why. It is desolate, flat, very windy and there is a nuclear power station in the distance along the coast that leads up to the lighthouse. What a strange place, I had never seen anything like it before. It wasn't "beachy" at all and my children were looking forward to a seaside trip that turned out to be more like visiting earth after an apocalypse.

This was hardly like Bali; no pool, no swaying palm trees, no surf, and the wind was blowing a very strong, southerly gale. This wasn't what the girls had in mind and while they tolerated us suggesting a walk up to the top of the lighthouse, they begrudgingly followed us inside the entry to the soaring structure with heavy feet.

They were quite taken by the lantern room where the lights were housed. The swirling colours of red, green, and white were a photo opportunity for them and they quickly uploaded artistic photos to social media. OK, this was going to be what our tourist status was all about, photo opportunities. Not just any old thing to take a photo of, but something unusual, something that said where you were, what you were doing, and if you could throw in some artistic licence then all the better. Unusual angles, photos from high up, low down, they were clicking away and sending them straight to the cloud for their friends to see. This was them keeping in touch with the other side of the world, and while they had access to great photo opportunities and Wi-Fi, we were going to be OK.

When Aurora and Coco were under the ages of ten, it was simple to go on holidays. If there was beach, a pool, or a water park, then we had hit the jackpot. They didn't need to be entertained, just let them swim all day and they would be happy, barely even getting out the water for food and extra sunscreen. Some days they were so water logged their skins starting peeling from the sheer amount of time spent in the water. They were just happy to be hanging around us and we weren't embarrassing to them.

Many days passed with me lying by the pool reading a plethora of books, whilst my husband suntanned to a darker shade of brown, occasionally double-checking the children were still in the pool. By the end of the day, they were both exhausted and promptly fell asleep leaving us with the night free.

Those days are gone.

Travelling with teenagers is whole different ballgame, lying by the pool and going to a water park all day isn't du jour anymore. Whilst they still do that in the climes of Bali, we weren't in Bali and there was no pool, just a vast expanse of pebbly beach, howling wind, and waves that limped into shore.

We asked them what they wanted to do while on holidays and "shopping" was the only answer. No, "I would love to see a historical city like Bath" or "I would love to visit a castle", just shopping. That was it.

"Are you sure there is nothing on your wish list here in the UK and Scotland?" I was somewhat stunned, it is a beautiful country with so many fascinating things to see and do, and they wanted to shop on the High Street.

Raymond said, "Your idea of a holiday is different to theirs, Jane."

I knew that, but I really wanted them to at least say, "I would like to see the Scottish Highlands."

Little did they know where I was planning to go was hardly a shopping mecca.

So how do we keep everyone happy? That question was harder than it sounded. We all loved different things, like most people do, but when you are a harmonious group of four (or so I thought through my rose coloured glasses) you would take it in turns. Do things that everyone liked, and then a few things that each other liked to do.

The problem was that everyone wanted to do different things.

We had limited time and limited money, we couldn't just take off and do the things that tugged at our heart's desires. You had to plan for some of those more popular experiences and the logistics of getting to them was proving to be difficult. So we had to make a plan. Out came the old fashioned map and the GPS instructions, and we figured out where we wanted to go—or not go as it turned out.

Several years ago in my usual way I announced to the family we were going to Austria to enjoy a white Christmas.

"Imagine the snow-capped mountains, the heavenly scent of gingerbread at the Christmas markets, and ice skating around with the snow falling gently on our eyelashes." I was so excited, but my children and husband didn't necessarily share my enthusiasm at the time. I had fallen into the trap before, creating my own family holidays in my mind and then making them a reality.

My visions were of waking up on Christmas morning and opening the windows to snow gently falling and the streets covered in beautifully made snowmen (and snowwomen). The stark reality was a lot different.

Suffice to say when we arrived in Vienna on 22 December for our white Christmas it had not been snowing at all. We were told it is "so unseasonal" for it not to be snowing. Great, I had hauled my children to the other side of the world to have a white Christmas and there was no snow.

On Christmas Eve we celebrated with our family friends, played music, and ate up a storm, but there was still no white stuff. Those pictures in my mind of waking up on Christmas morning were instead met with grey skies, drizzle, and a temperature hovering around four degrees. Nothing like I imagined. It was still lovely and we made the most of it, but I was a little disappointed.

I am not sure why I did it to myself, I should know better, but there I was, imagining again. Imagining how wonderful a family holiday would be, driving through the Scottish Highlands with the wind in our hair, and the faint sound of bagpipes in the distance.

I have watched Eurovision since I was a child—I remember ABBA winning in 1974. Every year since, I have tried my utmost to watch it, whichever country I happened to be in at the time. I was totally transfixed on this unfashionable show reel of performers from far flung countries that I couldn't pronounce. Imagine my delight when we arrived in the UK in 2017 just in time for the live finals, and in the right time zone for once. I had always woken at 5am (Australian time) to watch it unfold on the other side of the world. My friends call me a "Eurovision tragic" and I am OK with that.

I was excited to actually be in Europe for the Eurovision Contest. The show runs for close to four hours, and along with our friends we started preparing for the long night ahead. Coco came up with the idea of cooking something from each European country (although we didn't get to 43 culinary dishes), and our food section consisted of Italian bruschetta, Greek olives, French bread, German sausages, Swedish meatballs, and Austrian wafers—it was an odd medley of food but such a fun mishmash.

Australia was competing so of course we were supporting them, although you could argue we really shouldn't have been in it at all. It is the biggest show on Earth and I was giddy with anticipation of watching it live.

We all curled up on the lounge and strapped ourselves in for the nights' entertainment... and it didn't disappoint. It was as crazy and outlandish as ever, and I for one hope it continues for another sixty-one years. I love it!

We took time out to visit the open day of the Dover Royal National Lifeboat Institution (RNLI) Station, and they put on a terrific day (despite missing the typically Australian 'sausage sizzle' out the front, but I forgive them for that). The RNLI is one of the most remarkable and brilliant organisations. It is hard to believe they have been around for over 190 years. Founded in 1824, it is the oldest lifeboat service in the world and they have saved over 140,000 lives. The "sea dogs", as they are affectionately known, are mostly volunteers, which makes them even more awesome.

The bright orange lifeboats were easy to see and I guess when they are out at sea that's imperative. Apparently when Lego decided to design a model of one of their life boats they had to create a special orange brick to make sure it was the right shade. The RNLI also rescue animals, and in 2013 they launched 118 lifeboats to rescue horses, goats, cows, and even ferrets, I cannot think of a more worthy and admirable institution.

Kate very kindly said we could loan their car to do our driving tour of England and Scotland. It was a real bonus, not having to rent a car and pay insurance premiums to do so. We just had to put petrol in it and take off! How fabulous to be told the car we could loan was a Mercedes Benz convertible. Wow, we were quite chuffed, but the children were less than impressed when they saw the backseat—or should I say lack of. I didn't realise the two-door convertible had back seats smaller than the size of an iPad. It really was a two person car, but unless we were prepared to hire one, it was our only option.

We had a trial drive around the block and squeezed ourselves and a modest amount of luggage into the car, to get a feel of how we would manage over a seven day period. Thankfully it was quite roomy as it turned out. Not a great deal of luggage space in the boot but we borrowed (again!) from our friends some soft sided travel bags and a couple of "Hong Kong" shoppers and we were in business.

Two nights before we took off on our road trip Raymond and I went out for the night, just the two of us, and left our friends in charge of our teenage children. They were happy to have them, they love them and it was quite special to have one on one time, being Aurora and Coco's godmothers. They were going to make dinner together and eat in the "good room". With a menu planned, the girls helped with the food preparation whilst the corner stereo was cranked up to include rap songs from the nineties. With "Jump Around" blaring from the speakers, the cooking frenzy was underway.

I should mention here that my children are not handy in the kitchen. Their idea of setting the table is filling up the water jug, and as far as cooking, well the only thing that comes out of my kitchen from them is chocolate fudge slice. So, why is it when you are with friends, all of a sudden they are MasterChef contestants wheeling out a foray of kitchen talk and suggestions about garnishes? I really don't know where it came from; maybe they do watch what I am doing in the kitchen after all. Our friends of course thought it was fabulous and went on about what great apprentice chefs they were.

As they sat down for dinner, the talk around the table was about school and hobbies. Coco plays netball, and when she said, "Dad is the manager of my netball club" Jules gasped.

"What is a nipple club?" she asked.

Well you could imagine my children faces as they broke out in fits of laughter, their Australian accents had made a benign word rather different sounding. They all thought it was hilarious, and our friends were relieved Dad didn't manage such an infamous club!

CHAPTER 2 – LONDON

Before we hit the road to the northern counties and Scotland, we spent a day in old London town to get into the swing of being in all this Englishness. Given we were on the coast, London is an hour's train ride away. English trains really are quite marvellous (I'm sure that regular commuters may not agree) but the services are regular, inexpensive, and the trains are clean and manned by cheery conductors. We had opted for the "family rail card" at £30, which gave us one-third off adult fares and 60% off child fares. We could travel up and back on the high speed train from Folkestone to Kings Cross St Pancreas station for £47 for us all. Not bad. The only stipulation was we had to leave after 10am, which, given we had two teenagers in tow, wasn't a problem. It would have been more of a problem if we had to leave before 10am.

Our first trip to Folkestone Central Railway Station was rather chaotic as we not only got lost driving there; we had to park the car in a space that was made for a Fiat 500 not a Mercedes CLK230. All passengers had to alight before parking, otherwise they would have been trapped inside. Meanwhile for me, getting out of the driver's side made for a spine-twisting feat of gymnastics.

Unbeknownst to us, the pound coin had received a makeover earlier in the year, and there were now shiny new coins in circulation. Apparently it was the first major change to the £1 coin in thirty-three years. With twelve sides, it is said to be the most secure coin in the world against counterfeiting. Some of the new features included a hologram, which was great, but try putting one of those new coins in a parking meter. They don't work. You can only use the old £1 coins and given they were going out of circulation, they were hard to come by.

Suffice to say, I was extremely happy the person standing behind me had a few spares in his pocket. The generous gesture cemented my belief the English are some of the politest people on the planet.

We made it just in time for the 10.01am out of Folkestone. Once we were comfortably seated for the 55 minute journey, we talked about what we wanted to do in London for the day. Before we left, I had booked a couple of activities. I sometimes try to book things in advance if I can, not only because it makes the itinerary easier (prevents walking around in dazed confusion for the morning), it also means I can budget.

Our last visit to London was during a cold and wintry December, a far cry from the mild temperatures we had experienced thus far. That being said, any time of year in London has its charms, winter is all about Christmas and the lights on Oxford and Regent Streets, chestnuts roasting on the corners. In summer, people fill the parks, musical events, and Wimbledon.

What can I say about London that hasn't been said a million times before? London is so many things, you cannot even begin to explain it, so I won't, but I agree with Samuel Johnson, "you can never tire of London".

Every corner we turned around presented us with more wonderment; it was hard to keep swivelling our heads to see it all. It was a most wonderful mixture of new and old; boasting world famous landmarks and museums, endlessly magnificent architecture, and fascinating history. I was, and always will be, addicted to this gorgeous city.

I booked tickets for a walking tour called London Graffiti and Street Art. I would not have chosen the street art tour for myself, but it was an unexpected success. We met our guide at Aldgate East Tube (underground) Station and right away we could tell she was a dedicated sightseeing guide. She was covered in tattoos, dressed in torn black tights, a mini dress, and had flashes of coloured hair pulled up in dreadlocks. She looked right at home, the perfect person to take us around the sometimes seedy streets of East London. The woman had a loud voice (which I appreciated) and she really knew her stuff.

That area of London has an infamous past, with its colourful characters, fascinating architecture, and mysterious treasures. Today it is quite the melting pot of cultures and nationalities. Traditionally, this district of inner London, was working class and an area settled by a mixture of Irish, French Huguenot, Jewish, and Bangladeshi—all of which could still be felt. Run down and neglected in the early 80s, the East End was definitely starting to look up these days. Some areas were a little bit dodgy—judging by some unsavoury characters lurking in the shadows—so I was happy we had a local on board to navigate the darkened lane ways.

I cannot say that walking down little cobblestone streets in search of street art has been in my top ten "things to do before I die", but it was hugely educational and enjoyable. Some of the artwork is nothing short of spectacular. I don't pretend to know anything about those talented artists, but if I saw them on a gallery wall I would be impressed. Given that they had rough surfaces and tiny spaces to work with, they would give mainstream artists a run for their money.

Our tour group was not large so we didn't take up too much room on the pavement, making it easy to stand and listen to our guide. She had quite the arsenal of facts and figures (many I cannot remember), but one that I do was about the little sculpture faces. I believe the artist is anonymous, and the little faces pop up on the sides of walls, doors, and alcoves. They are sometimes a bit grotesque but others are sweet and painted in muted colours. They are not easy to find so our guide had us on the hunt for them and Coco was quite apt at finding them, along with the street signs that had extra little people or animals.

They looked like normal road signs until you look a bit closer. It was a great exercise in realising we take everything around us for granted, but delve a little deeper and open your eyes, and you will find magic.

The children were mesmerised by these striking works of art and the stealth in which they were painted. Many of the artists' work under the darkness of night, or the anonymity of nameless attribute, giving the art the air of lawlessness and danger. The artists sneak around in the dark alleys of East London in pursuit of the perfect wall or door to express themselves on. It really is quite wonderful, and I hope they continue to adorn the walls of laneways and alleys for years to come.

The weather started to turn about halfway through our tour, which was unfortunate as we were not really prepared for soggy weather (I know, we were in England, we should carry an umbrella and raincoat at all times!). We did have hoods so we spent the last hour peeking out from under our cloaks, looking more and more like drowned rats. My boots started squishing by the time the tour ended. It didn't deter me, but we were happy when we finished up at the Spitafields Market, which was warm and dry.

The markets live in the heart of the East End and has a history dating back to 1666. Apparently traders had started setting up there after the Great Fire of London. Amazing. The success of the market encouraged people to settle there and it grew in popularity. Since the 1970s a flourishing Bangladeshi community has blossomed, bringing new businesses and the famous Brick Lane restaurant district. We stayed indoors under the expansive roof and ate pancakes and drank hot chocolate, completely soaked to the bone.

We caught the tube back to Green Park but unfortunately the rain hadn't subsided as we popped our heads up from the underground stairs, it was drizzly in the way that just makes you wet.

Since a walk in the park was out of the question, we decided on a different mode of transport that didn't involve being outdoors. One of the best ways to get around is on one of London's famous red buses. Not the tourist ones, just the normal route masters.

They are all double-decker and my children absolutely loved heading straight up the stairs and taking the very front seats. They give you a bird's eye view of not only all the sights but the tops of people's heads (well the tops of umbrellas today). We hopped on route nine and seated ourselves on the top deck ready for a trip through the Monopoly board. The windows were fogged up and the girls proceeded to draw smiley faces on the glass (previous occupants of the front seat had done similar things by the look of it, I'm sure I saw some love hearts). It was respite from the rain and very comfortable so I was content to stay there for quite some time, letting someone else drive.

The route meandered around London's ancient streets and took us past some famous landmarks: Hyde Park, Royal Albert Hall, Harrods, Palace Gate, Kensington Palace, the Design Museum, and Warwick Gardens, to name a few. It was the London we all saw in movies and television shows ... you could spend a lifetime exploring it.

I believe the best way to explore anywhere is on foot. You

obviously don't cover as much ground on foot, but you really get the feeling of a place when you walk it. Suffice to say, it is only suitable when your children are over the age of ten. It gives you the opportunity to stop anywhere, take in the surrounds, or grab an ice cream. Teenagers are robust in this sense, they are used to walking, they don't have a driver's licence (yet!), so it is their only method besides public transport. Using a bit of both works well. When we travelled to New York City the previous year, we would walk along Riverside Park for about ten blocks, then duck along 79th to catch the subway. We would pop out the other end and then walk along the Highline, the perfect blend of walking and mass transit.

It was a little more challenging to walk in England as we didn't have a nifty subway system handy. We balanced the two by driving to a destination and then walking the towns, villages, churches, and medieval streets. It worked well, (in London, at least) and we didn't hear the words "my legs are tired" once. I suspect if I had suggested a walk up the 528 steps to the Gallery of St Paul's Cathedral, they would have politely declined. So would I, come to think of it.

It is enviable you will get lost sometimes on holiday. It is not a bad thing, I believe you really don't know a place until you do get lost. That is when you discover the most unexpected things. To me, it is the real meaning of wanderlust, and I am the queen of getting lost. It's not that I do it on purpose, it just seems to happen. I have little spatial awareness and I cannot read maps (my husband will concur with me on this). So while I am standing on street corner turning the map this way and that, loudly pronouncing we need to go "this way", nine times out of ten, it is completely the wrong direction. If I am with Raymond, he will correct me and save us heading in the opposite direction to where we were supposed to be going. My children get exasperated with me at home when I am driving and abruptly pull up because I am lost. I seem to particularly do this on a Sunday. Coco says, "Are you lost, Mum? Oh, it's Sunday, of course you are!"

These days with smart phones it is almost impossible to get lost, but I still manage to. I have a few apps on my phone that give directions and even spell it out for you, tell you exactly where to go (of course in the nicest possible way). But I also trust my instincts and just wander, which is met with the usual eye roll from my children who like things to be a bit more structured. I am slowly turning them around to my way of thinking and living on the edge for a while, it's quite liberating. Getting out of your comfort zone is a must every now and again. It builds character, confidence, and resilience. From a young age we are almost inbuilt with the notion that to be lost is scary and daunting, but it can be the opposite, it can be enlightening.

Scary movies play on that notion, the heroine at some point always seems to be wandering around in the dark, lost and confused. Being lost is synonymous with being frightened, when what we should do is embrace being lost and look for the surprises that we are inevitably going to encounter. Just saying.

Things also go wrong. It is inevitable. You cannot always control each day and life has a way of making its own plans, call it the universe or Mother Nature, both will interrupt your perfect travel plans.

The weather is an obvious one, but unless you are caught in a cyclone, you and your children will cope with walking in the rain, sleet, sun, or wind. The weather shouldn't prevent you from doing anything. What is more of a bother is if you lose something. Over the years of travel, that has happened to us on more than one occasion.

Several years back, we travelled to Venice with the children in January. It was as magical as I remembered on a previous visit, some fourteen years before. We were there at the same time of year, which in my mind is a perfect time to visit Venice. It may be on the chilly side, but there are no crowds, smelly lagoons, or cruise ships. It is the Venice you imagine in your dreams; the sky is crystal clear and blue, even though the temperature is hovering around five degrees. There was still a festive feel in the air in early January, the fairy lights were strung between medieval buildings and the gorgeous little bridges were adorned with flowers and red ribbons. As it gets dark so early, it is the perfect light show during an afternoon walk in search of beautiful Italian food.

Getting around in Venice is easy, you just hop on the vaporetto, the Venetian version of public transport: water buses. It really is the best way to get to each area you are visiting. After a day of sightseeing, we caught the vaporetto back to our hotel. As we alighted and watched it chug away, we realised we had left one of our travelling bags on board. Well, panic ensued; this was the bag with the cakes in it! Aurora and Coco were not worried about anything else in the bag, which contained, guidebooks, maps, hats, gloves, ear muffs, and scarves, but thankfully no money or passports.

I really wasn't that keen on having to replace these items, and given the weather was cold and we still had weeks left of our trip, we couldn't be without our winter woollies. The girls had been given celebration cakes as we left Austria the day before. They were special celebration cakes from Epiphany, and they were saving them to eat when we got back to the hotel. They were upset, they were the prettiest little cakes and all done up in ribbon. I, on the other hand, was frantically trying to work how (in my broken Italian) to contact the Azienda del Consorzio Trasporti Veneziano to find out if someone had handed our bag in.

We headed up to the transport hub to enquire but were told that they wouldn't know until the end of the day when the vaporetto all came in after their day out. We had no choice but to head back to our accommodation and wait for a call… or not.

We arrived at our hotel and told the concierge what happened. They were upbeat about our belongings coming back to us, so that buoyed our mood. We set out into the night for an Italian dinner and tried not to think about it too much. Imagine our surprise when we returned after dinner to be told our bag had been handed in and we could collect it the next day. Sometimes things have a way of coming back to you, but in this case it was sans celebration cakes, much to the dismay of the children.

This part of London is good looking, fashionable, and a bit quirky. It houses Liberty, the world famous department store, and Carnaby Street, two distinctly different retail experiences.

I headed into Liberty, Aurora and Coco headed towards Carnaby Street. The weather was still on the soggy side and I was keen to stay undercover as much as possible. I remember the first time I entered Liberty in the 1990's, it was like entering an eastern bazaar, a marketplace full of trinkets, jewellery, curios, homewares, knick knacks, and the famous "liberty" prints. It still has a whimsical and creative feel about it, and is the most unexpected place. You could spend hours there poking around and exploring all the separate rooms.

I was quite amazed to read that Liberty was constructed from the timber of two English ships—how extraordinary!

Raymond stood patiently outside a trendy fashionista store on Carnaby Street for almost an hour waiting for the girls, and the look on his face was one of weary disillusionment. He is about as excited about shopping as me, and suffice to say we were both in need of a decent drink.

CHAPTER 3 – HITTING THE ROAD

One real bonus about a driving holiday in the UK is they drive on the same side of the road as us. This is fortuitous, I have gone around a roundabout the wrong way in Germany, because it feels unnatural to be driving on the right side of the road. I was rather surprised to learn only 35% of the world's population drives on the left, and they are mainly old British colonies. Apparently there is good reason, and it dates back to feudal times. Since most people were right handed, swordsman preferred to keep to the left so they could keep their right arm closer to their opponent, ready to brandish their swords in combat. Left handed driving was made mandatory in Britain in 1853, and countries such as Australia followed suit. Today, only four European countries drive on the left: United Kingdom, Ireland, Cyprus, and Malta and I was happy that I didn't need to constantly check the parked cars to remember what side of the street I should be driving on.

Day one of the driving holiday had arrived. We planned to get an early start, but with two teenagers on board the words "early start" were not going to be part of our vocabulary for the next seven days. Note to self: do not organise any activities in the morning. Teenagers and early morning starts don't mix, not unless you want moody and surly backseat passengers for the rest of the day.

I had to allow time for them to not only get up and find their clothes amongst the ever growing pile tossed on the floor but for them to expertly do their hair and make-up. It takes hours for make-up application to look like they are not wearing any makeup. Go figure, how about just not wearing any makeup at all? Then we could leave two hours earlier. The girls had packed all sorts of makeup, hair accessories, and appliances; one would think we were going to the back of beyond, not first world countries where all of these things are available. Half of their suitcases were taken up by sets of brushes, eyebrow pencils, and moisturisers. I am not sure why they had to haul all these beauty products to the other side of the world, what would have been sensible was to bring the basics, buy some stuff here, and ditch it when we left. But no, all their favourites had to come on holidays with us. I clearly don't have any idea (so I was told) about the importance of an eyelash curler!

By 10am we were ready to go. We waved to our friends from the driveway as we reversed out into the street with a Priscilla Queen of the Desert farewell—I wanted to smash a champagne bottle over the front bumper bar, but sadly that got vetoed.

We mapped out our journey, and had booked accommodation in Bath, Somerset. We factored in a bit of traffic but I loudly announced it would take us no more than four hours, and we would stop in and check out Stonehenge on the way. Perfect. Itinerary sorted. We jumped on the motorway and headed west.

The first hour we drove through the bottom of Kent along the motorway and passed rolling hills and Oasthouses, how very British. Stonehenge was on the M3, which intersected with the M25 and the GPS was pointing us in the right direction. A few miles on and there were signs everywhere about a diversion on the M3. Okay... we just had to keep an eye out for that and we would head around the diversion.

Several hours later, and three aborted attempts to get onto the M3 – we were defeated. We couldn't find the road, and were just going around in circles. We had so many instances of déjà vu we were starting to wonder if we had somehow ended up in Alice in Wonderland. I was driving by that stage, and I was starting to become quite vocal in the front seat about our lack of direction and the time it was taking to get to our destination.

As I looked in the review mirror, both girls had their heads down, staring at their phones with ear buds in and no idea of what was going on outside the car.

I said, "I'm sorry girls but we are just going to have to go straight to Bath, we won't be able to see Stonehenge after all."

Coco replied after taking one ear bud out, "That's fine, Mum. It's just a bunch of old rocks, we didn't want to go anyway."

While I was happy we didn't have to pay the exorbitant entry fee to get into Stonehenge, it did make me re-think some of the attractions I was planning to visit. I had tried to include the girls in the holiday planning, I had read 'involving your teen in trip planning is key', but what if they don't give you any answers? What if they just shrug their shoulders and say, "Whatever"?

Trying to engage them to suggest at least one thing each was exhausting. I never got an answer, so it was down to me again to decide what we visited each day.

Before we left, I trawled through the library in the sky to gain wisdom and insight on travelling with teenagers. According to the travel channel, 'The key to successfully travelling with your teenagers, lies in what you do before you get on the aeroplane.'

To be honest, there wasn't much to read, there was lot about travelling with babies and under-fives, but little on the next stages of your children's life. I had been there done that with the under-five age group, I however was intrigued by one hint: "Bring a friend". What the? Bring another two teenagers? You have got to be joking. I was struggling with the concept of travelling with my own two teenagers let alone someone else's. I was aiming for a peaceful and happy vacation, and when the teenagers outnumber the parents that just might be a recipe for disaster. Anyhow, four were not going to fit in the backseat of the Mercedes.

Another 'hint' was encouraging your teenager to write in a travel journal. I have adopted this practice practically all my life. I love writing and spent my childhood holidays scribbling in notebooks, sticking scrap pieces of paper in the margins, folding articles into the sleeve, flattening flowers, seeds, and bark into the pages, drawing pictures, and trying to stuff as many mementos of my holiday into an A5 sized book. By the end of the holiday it was bulging with everything I had collected, including what turned out to be a very smelly starfish.

Is that sort of enthusiasm taught? I think it may be innate, I was born with that ability, but could I pass it on to my children, like wanderlust? I was not sure. Over the years I encouraged both my children to keep a travel journal and while the first few days of our vacation there were a flurry of writing, by the third day it had all but been abandoned and thrown into the bottom of the suitcase. In these modern times, all of that and more can be stored in a smart phone, no need to write anything. This old fashioned skill is distinctly becoming out of fashion.

A lot of the literature I read about travelling with teenagers had suggestions of destinations that would be favoured by your child. It included 'Club Holidays', with a range of activities like tennis, golf, water sports, and—wait for it—archery and paintballing. I'm not sure I would get that holiday across the line with the children; they don't exactly need to burn off excess energy. Cruises are another favourite apparently, mainly because there are so many activities available, you can prepay and there are teen-only lounge areas and dances. 'The biggest bonus is the all hours, unlimited access to food'. I cannot say that sailing out into the open ocean has been a life long desire of mine, so that one wouldn't pass my criteria, quite frankly (although the all-you-can eat option sounds like it would have saved my credit card blow outs). I have friends who love cruising with their children, and family members who book annual cruises, but I'd pass on that one.

Not one article said travelling around England and Scotland in a sports car was a number one choice when teenagers were asked, "If you could go anywhere in the world, where would it be?"

I did actually ask my children that question (though I knew the answer) and they said Bali, where they could sit by the pool for a week, lie around beach clubs, and shop at flea markets. The word compromise was going to be part of my vocabulary for the next week.

Several weeks before we arrived in the UK, I had been out dancing with my girlfriends. I love a boogie and when you can let your hair down with friends, even better. I jumped, twirled, and twisted my way around the dance floor, and thought I was doing an excellent impersonation of Tina Turner. We drank sparkling wine in between dance numbers and had a whale of a time.

The next morning I woke up with not only a raging hangover, but I could barely roll out of bed. Every one of my intercostal muscles was on fire. I had mistakenly thought I was twenty years younger the night before, and busted out moves that are not conducive to a woman in her late forties. I creaked, literally. My ribs were so painful I had to roll to one side just to get out of bed, and stretching up to do anything was near on impossible. By the time I had to slip into a two-door Mercedes, my injuries had subsided but not completely disappeared. This made for a slightly painful entry and exit out of the driver's seat. I was determined not to let my mood (or holiday) be spoilt by a few niggling rib muscles, suffice to say I kept a tube of Dencorub nearby at all times. This made for a slightly interesting smell in the Mercedes – a mixture of football locker room and coffee.

Not a scent I would suggest as an air freshener.

CHAPTER 4 - BATH

It was well after 6pm when we arrived in our accommodation on the outskirts of Bath. It had taken us twice as long to do the trip—so much for my four hours.

I was in desperate need of an alcoholic beverage. We had seven days to do our road trip, and I wanted to get as far north as Inverness. It wasn't looking too promising going on the outcome of today's driving. It had taken us all day to drive 290 kilometres –at that rate we would not be getting very far on our family road trip of a lifetime!

First stop was the local pub, and thank goodness for the British pub! What an institution. I loved it, right at that moment I couldn't think of anywhere else I would rather be. The weather had turned rather drizzly by that stage and there was a definite dense fogginess to the air–the perfect night to be in a pub, eating chicken schnitzel, and drinking of pint of beer.

Pub names in England are hilarious–I absolutely love them. We have nothing like it at home. Names like, 'Rat & Parrot', 'Pig & Fiddle', and my favourite, 'The Shoulder of Mutton'. How the pubs got their names is interesting as it turns out, their names were often chosen by what was easier to illustrate. Going back hundreds of years, the customers would have been largely illiterate, so they had to draw the pictures for their signs so the patrons could recognise which pub was which.

Alehouses, taverns, and inns became collectively known as public houses (shortened to pub) around the reign of King Henry VII, but throughout history it was thought that beer and ale have been a staple part of the British diet, due to the fact that it was safer than drinking water at the time.

I love the fact pubs are such social places, with the gatherings of family and friends to relax and enjoy each other's company. I had read recently that there had been a decline in 'pub culture', but on this driving holiday, we would take full advantage of this most wonderful British institution. It was the first of many pubs we visited over the seven days.

Our accommodation in Bath was from the road a grand looking old farmhouse, and on closer inspection was very appealing. It was built in the 1600's and originally used as a reposing house for monks on their pilgrimages between Glastonbury and Malmesbury.

Our family room was spacious, and there was plenty of room to spread ourselves out. After a challenging day navigating the English road system, I would have been happy to sleep on the floor, my eyes were sore from trying to read contradictory motorway signs, and I may have had one too many beers at the pub.

We woke the next morning to a brilliant blue sky and emerald green, rolling hills. How quintessentially British. I loved the countryside, it is perfect in every way. England somehow manages to fit into its 'island' space the most magnificent array of countryside, whether it is green rolling hills dotted with black and white cows, rugged crops of mountains with stone facing sides, or lavender filled moors. I never tire of seeing such beauty.

I said to the girls, "Look out the window this morning, isn't it beautiful?"

"Yes, Mum, whatever you say..."

Well, at least I got a response.

We headed downstairs for breakfast and were greeted with another British institution: the English breakfast. We chose whatever we wanted from bacon, eggs, baked beans, mushrooms, hash browns... and the list goes on. The girls eyes lit up, hash browns for breakfast! I had resigned myself to the fact I needed to compromise with food on this trip.

> *'Don't stress if your teenager isn't as keen to experience new food as much as you are, even cheese on toast and hot dogs can turn into memorable meals'.*

It wasn't about the food we were eating, it was about the experience of being together as a family and sharing stories over the breakfast/dinner table. We were going to be eating out a lot, so I wanted those dining experiences to be about being together, and not a discussion about the healthy options on the menu.

When Coco gave me the blank gaze and shrugged her shoulders when I asked what she wanted to eat, "I dunno, I'm not that hungry", I could have the argument about being able to make simple food choices, or just ignore the attitude and order what I wanted. I decided if she didn't order when I did, well that's too bad, she could go hungry. I wasn't bothered. Making a scene in the restaurant was not worth it and did not add to the ambience.

They learnt quickly it was not like home, there was no pantry for snacking, and food stops had to be timed when available in the schedule. We would not be stopping every hour, on the hour, for food. They worked it out in the end, stock up on food when you have the chance and eat a good breakfast! We battled a bit to begin with, but it sorted itself out and we started to relax at meal times and enjoy ourselves.

Experiencing that part of grown up life is important. Eating out at restaurants is a skill you don't always think about, especially if you don't eat out that much. How to conduct yourself in a restaurant is important, some would say imperative.

As we sat there, waiting for our breakfast, the family greyhound arrived and put its head on our table. Well Aurora and Coco thought it was gorgeous, finally something they were excited about! A dog at the breakfast table... whoever would have thought two teenage girls would be excited to be sharing their meal with a furry friend? Raymond and I paled into insignificance as we ate our breakfast, watching our children feeding the dog from the table.

Bath is a UNESCO world heritage site that reflects two great eras in English history, Roman and Georgian. You would be hard pressed to find a more grand city than Bath, it is quite stunning as you come down the hill, laid out in all is splendour, awash with glowing honey coloured stone. The morning sun catches the light perfectly. It is an architectural gem, full of gorgeous buildings, all shapes and sizes, the most famous being curved.

Royal Crescent is a must see, built by John Wood the Younger between 1767 – 1774 it is the grandest of Bath's many Georgian crescents with views over the Royal Victoria Park. Bath Circus is my favourite, designed by John Wood the Elder, the houses form a circle built in three sections facing onto a central green. The houses are decorated with stone carvings and columns, and no two houses are the same. We spent quite some time looking at the intricate and delicate stonework.

Like Florence in Italy, Bath has a shop lined bridge called Pulteney Bridge which has been built over the River Avon. It is full of tiny little shops including cafés and antiques. It had a very good view back over the terraced Pulteney Weir. The day we were there, many people milled around as street buskers set up for the day. We grabbed a lunch on the go, which was packaged in a small paper bag, including a sandwich, cookie, drink, and piece of fruit. Very handy, and I quite liked the concept of being able to walk and eat and the same time.

We took the free guided tour run by members of the council. It was a great bonus to get a two hour guided walk through Bath with a local for free! I was amazed at how many people turned up outside the Pump Rooms to join the tour. Thankfully there were four guides and we were broken off into groups of about fifteen, which meant I could at least hear what the guide was saying.

I love walking tours, they are much better than the hop-on hop-off bus trips, and not only do you get to see everything at ground level, you have an experienced local who is passionate about their city/town and they want you to love it as much as they do.

Our guide for the two hours had lived in Bath all her life, and was a tiny bit theatrical but nonetheless engaging and knowledgeable. She also had a loud voice that I very much appreciated, this seemed to be a re-occurring theme with our guides.

It was a beautiful spring day in Bath and the muted stone that adorned practically every building was glowing in this morning sun, all warm and gold. It must be said that it's a very handsome city, not only its beautiful Roman Baths, circuses, and churches but every little home, footpath, garden, and shop kept with the architecture of the day. It was so neat and tidy and quintessentially English. You could not mistake the city to be in any other country but England.

As we made our way through the square at the front of the Bath Abbey, our guide explained some of the adornments on the front. If you look closely, you can see little angels climbing up long ladders, and it has been said (by our guide) the olive tree and crown carving was for the Bishop of Bath, Oliver King, a sort of picture story of his name, a bit like the pub illustrators but carved in stone.

Coco answered our guide's question regarding the symbols for the olive tree and the crown—she was listening after all. Amazingly, there was so much to see just on the front of the Abbey, let alone inside.

The sun made the buildings sparkle in that morning glow way and the town centre of Bath was humming and buzzing predominately with tourists—it was a Sunday after all. Just walking these ancient streets is a wonder, the fact that Romans walked them thousands of years ago to come and splash around in the healing waters of the thermal spas, was quite incredible. The Roman Baths and Temple complex have been redesigned throughout the centuries, and now houses a modern roof top wellness spa. We could make out white robed patrons swanning around on the balconies, with quite the queue at the door. Our shorts and t-shirts were in contrast to that scene on the upper floors, as we shuffled along the cobblestones. Yet it was perfect weather for walking, and it suited me better to be out and about in nature, admiring the beautiful architecture. I'm sure my children felt otherwise.

Another great part about a walking tour is you get to see a lot in a fairly short period of time, just enough to get the feel of a place, but not too long that your teenagers are rolling their eyes and asking, "When are we going?"

Keeping on the move is imperative to keep up the enthusiasm (or lack of when you stop for too long).

The red telephone box is an icon of Britain; loved by many they are instantly recognisable. Perfect for photo opportunities and social media status. Aurora and Coco took the chance to break away from the tour for a few minutes to take action shots in the cast iron kiosks. The photos are delightful and fun, I smiled and joined in the fun.

There is a lot to see in Bath and we managed to see quite a bit.

Not only did we see the royal crescent, Circus, and Bath Abbey, but Sally Lunn's house, the oldest house in Bath which was built in 1482. Sally Lunn lived there in the late 1600s and began baking the (now) world famous Bath bun which are still baked and served on the premises. The buns are light and airy, like sweet brioche.

It was all about proper English tea there too. You could have morning tea, lunch, or afternoon tea. Quite delicious. Another must is Prior Park which is a beautiful 18th century landscaped garden, restored by the National Trust and features a palladian bridge, a lake, and views over Bath. It was partly designed by Capability Brown, the landscape architect who seemed quite prolific in the green spaces of the English countryside.

The Jane Austen Centre in Bath is a unique centre that explores the life of Jane Austen, the famous novelist who was a resident of Bath during Georgian times. The centre gives you a snapshot of her life and how living in Bath affected her writing. She lived in Bath for only five years, but remained a frequent visitor. Her likeness is still there today in the vast amount of souvenir themed merchandise. Not a bad thing I guess, to get young people interested in classic literature. Northhanger Abbey by Jane Austen is one of my favourites. Catherine the main character in the book, is my kind of gal.

The other big change since my visit in 1998 is the internet. Back in the nineties it was in its infancy, and nothing like what it is today. The library in the sky is truly amazing and no more so than for the purpose of travelling in another country. The accommodation websites are so user friendly, offering affordable and convenient lodgings around the world. It was helpful to have this service available at our fingertips. In 1998 you had to book weeks in advance (sometimes months), and all you had to go on was an endorsement in a travel guide with very little in the way of photos or recommendations. It was unheard of to see pictures of the rooms, or comments about the service or cleanliness (or lack of!) of the property. It was a wing it and a pray scenario, you took your chances and if the hotel/B&B or guest house was far from satisfactory, you had nowhere to voice your opinion and no chance of ever getting a refund.

In 2017 you could browse properties, check out reviews, and have a sneak peek inside the rooms before you even contemplated booking. We enthusiastically used these websites, and found the most interesting places that were not only memorable, but fitted nicely into our travel budget.

When we arrived at our night's camp we would prop ourselves up with a glass of wine, and search the possible offerings for the next stopover. It was so much fun and we really hit the jackpot, we stayed in some of the most unforgettable places (wonderful inspiration for this book!).

CHAPTER 5 – COTSWOLDS AND HAMSTALL RIDWARE

The next morning we headed up the A40 towards the Cotswolds. The area is such a magical part of the UK, it is quintessentially British, with its chocolate box cottages and postcard-worthy villages. We wanted to show the girls this unspoilt and historic corner of England.

We decided to visit Chipping Norton first. This market town in the Cotswolds is perfectly preserved and has a long high street, flanked by golden stone buildings that settle a yellow glow over the town. It was quite busy there, bus loads of tourists were being offloaded near the town hall, and as we parked our car in the central median strip, we were already searching for a café. I hadn't had a coffee that morning and I was in desperate need of a caffeine hit.

We happened across a delightful little laneway with hanging planters full of happily coloured pansies next to the Lygon Arms pub that had outdoor seating and served coffee. We spent a good hour there sipping coffee and taking in the very pleasant morning sunshine. The courtyard was quiet and off the main street, which was lovely. Birds chirped and everything in the world was good. I was going to enjoy this trip immensely—it would be a trip we would remember. My heart was singing.

After our coffee we pottered about looking in the windows of shops and just soaking in the atmosphere. There was the usual array of giftware stores, selling everything from artwork to tea towels, with pretty tea rooms but there were also the 'working' type of shop too, which sold everything from hardware to plant seedlings. Some of the gift shops had their wares outside on the pavement and we browsed along the steps and commented on some of the wooden wall hangings like, 'Stay safe, eat cake'. I'm not even sure what that means, or where you would hang such an item. Raymond especially liked the one that said, "Rules for dating my daughter" and in case you want to know, these are a few:

Understand I don't like you.
I'm everywhere.
You hurt her, I hurt you.
Be home 30 minutes early.
Get a lawyer.
If you lie, I will find out.
I don't mind going back to jail.

Phew, that sounds like something out of a Liam Neeson movie! We had a laugh and I promised the children Dad wouldn't buy it and hang it on the front door.

I read that, 'Teenagers sporadically get into hermit mode', which I knew this well from life at home. Aurora particularly likes being a recluse in her bedroom on the weekends. She needs her space, and that is why she has the bedroom at the far end of the house (hermit time, not to be confused with hammer time). She loves her own company, which is a skill I do not have.

Coco and I love being around people, we get energy from others and genuinely want to spend time with our fellow human beings. The concept of alone time is foreign to me, but I had to think about it a lot on the trip, the children were definitely happier when we balanced the time we spent together, and the time we spent apart. It wasn't always possible as we were constantly on the move, but whenever we arrived earlier than expected, I made a point of letting them hang out in the room or pub while Raymond and I went for a walk (and searched for coffee). It suited us all, we got to explore the local area without their exasperated tones about our penchant for history and culture and they got to take selfies and post them on their social pages. Win-win in my book. The compromise worked well, and we never got the, "I'm tired of castles and churches" speech.

Leaving the unique and magnificent Cotswolds behind us, we headed for the Peak District via the M5 motorway past Birmingham to a very small village called Hamstall Ridware... and when I say small, I mean small. Less than four hundred people live there. It has three streets, a church, and a pub and that's about it. It is all but a tiny blip on the map, a blink and you would miss it type of village. But I was keen to visit some of these off the beaten track places too, there are so many beautifully preserved English villages and towns dotted all over of the country, but they have tourists swarming in them in the warmer months. While certainly worthwhile, I needed to see some of the more forgotten places that weren't on the tourist trail and were in need of our patronage.

The road leading into the village had room for only one car and was boarded by hedgerows, which made it impossible to see if anything was coming the other way. We didn't encounter any traffic thankfully and made our way to our accommodation for the night. By that stage it was getting late, and according to the girls the drive had been, "boring", which I must say was fairly close to the truth. The M5 is hardly spectacular scenery driving.

Our accommodation was a family room above the pub and it was really rather good. We hadn't stayed in that many pubs over the years but it was pretty much the only accommodation in town and they also served food, which is a bonus when the nearest place to eat was not within walking distance.

The English weather was turning out to be on our side, with the afternoon sun warm, and the night mild with very little breeze. We had all the windows and doors open, and the feint smell of sheep poo drifted through our back door.

When Aurora and Coco ventured outside to the back of the pub they squealed with delight at the four baby lambs, running around the back paddock adjoined to the pubs beer garden. In fact, all that backed onto the pub was green fields and agricultural machinery, we were definitely in the countryside there.

The spring lambs were only a week old, they had gorgeous little faces and black and white bodies with flapping tails. The girls thought they were the cutest things they had ever seen, and I agreed.

Aurora and Coco are city girls, they had grown up in the suburbs of Melbourne, with no access to farm animals on a day to day basis so they both rushed to the back fence to pat the lambs and take endless amounts of videos and photos of the lambs running circles around the paddocks.

Coco declared she wanted one as a pet so I had to explain they don't stay that size and were usually bred to eat. That didn't go down too well.

The pubs' beer garden also had swings and an old fashioned ten pin bowling floor, complete with bowling balls and skittles. Raymond and Coco tried their luck at bowling, whilst Aurora swung from the ropes of the swing attached to the boughs of the large oak trees.

What a gorgeous sight; green rolling hills, twilight, spring lambs, and family doing outdoorsy things. It was something to treasure.

The scene before me was what I like to call, 'living more life'. It was being present, and taking in the inspirational world around us. It was the main reason I wanted to do this trip with my children, to experience life and hold the memories close to our hearts. It sounds corny, I know, but it has been said that when humans near the end of their lives, their biggest regret is not spending time with their children and family. I didn't want to regret that. We had a window of opportunity whilst the children were still in our care and living at home, but as teenagers, we had little time left for family holidays. We were well aware our children would probably not want to be holidaying with the "olds" by the time they are eighteen, they will want to be travelling with their friends to far flung places and sunny beach destinations—not the middle of country England—although I have been told if we're paying, they will happily come with us.

As the sun sunk behind the hills, we headed into the pub for a drink, and the children went upstairs to have valuable 'downtime', AKA disappearing into their devices. It was their holiday as much as ours, and we were entering that time zone opportunity of them being able to talk in real time to their friends in Australia.

Raymond and I perched ourselves on two bar stools and ordered the local beer. It was sometime after 8pm and pretty much right on cue, the locals starting arriving for their after dinner night cap. It was obviously a ritual, and one I liked very much. Whether it be to catch up with friends and neighbours, have an alcoholic beverage, or just needing to get out of the house, the pub was a sanctuary for many. It keeps us interacting with fellow human beings, it creates familiarity, prevents loneliness, gathers community spirit. The pub ritual has many faces, all so worthwhile in any town or village, whether it be 40,000 people or less than 400... and what a gathering we had that Sunday night.

Our accents gave us away as 'foreigners', and we were the centre of attention. Where are you from? Why are you visiting here?

The list of questions was endless, but I loved it. I loved talking to all those strangers, people from many walks of life in that tiny village. Some had been born there, and still lived and worked there. I was very interested to know what people do in such a village and they had many talents; carpenters, bakers, farmers, kindergarten teachers, and some had retired there for the quiet country life. How marvellous.

We learnt about the history of this quaint little town (probably too much from the publican, if I admit) but the locals wanted us to know about their families and their histories in this neck of the woods, which was fascinating, considering they have records from hundreds of years ago. If you were doing a family tree it would be most helpful, we however, were not. We enjoyed our evening in the pub, good food, excellent beer, and wonderful conversations with strangers.

Those are the times when you have faith in human nature, the sense of community, camaraderie. Whatever is going on in the world makes no difference to this tiny piece of England, where life is perfect, and has been forever.

The next day we headed for the Lake District via the Peak District. Two very magnificent national parks and I was keen to show Aurora and Coco the green rolling hills of England. Those are the views we all see on TV and in the movies, I wanted them to experience just how awe-inspiring nature can be, and that morning it was putting on pretty good show. The sun was out, the birds were chirping, and we took the roof off the convertible for the 'wind in our hair' experience.

It started well as we wound our way through the tiny laneways, criss-crossing the countryside with the BBC Radio 2 blaring old 80s tunes, which I was happily singing along to, much to the disdain of my teenagers.

My singing was interrupted with choruses of, "Mum, it is too windy in the back seat!"

"We cannot hear a thing, and my hair is getting messed up."

My answer to all that was, "Put a hat on!"

I absolutely loved winding my way up and down the most picturesque part of the world. Every corner turned presented us with more beauty. I had never seen such stunning scenery and it was breathtaking to see it in real life and not just on the screen while watching Pride and Prejudice. I wish I had taken more photographs but I didn't stop the car enough to take photos of the sweeping hillsides with their rocky outcrops. I know better for next time.

I shouted from the front seat, "Wow, girls, isn't this awesome?"

They looked up over their smart phones briefly with a vague, "Yeah, Mum, whatever" and promptly put their heads down again. I couldn't make sense of how they could not be totally blown away by Mother Nature.

"Can you put the roof up, Mum? It's too cold and windy, and I think I have something in my eye."

So much for the 'wind in our hair' experience. It lasted all of forty minutes.

My children were past the age of playing 'I spy', but as that part of the trip was becoming rather boring we decided a quick game may be in order. It always starts relatively well, but ends up with Coco guessing correctly all of our 'I spy' combinations, and then we run out of ideas. When it's her turn to give us an object, she chooses something so obscure there is no chance we could ever guess.

"I spy with my little eye, something beginning with CP." (2 words).

Well we guess and guess and guess, we even ask her for clues, but we are defeated.

So what is something that starts with a C and a P?

Cow poo.

I'm suspicious she could have spied cow poo from the back window of the Mercedes but the game was short lived and the children retreated back into their devices, listening to music.

Raymond and I chatted in the front seat, in the very conversational way that ends up with me just raving on about nothing in particular. He nods and agrees with me, but I suspect if I asked him ten minutes later what I was talking about, he would not remember. I was just white noise, and I was okay with that. I'm known to be very fond of my own voice.

Raymond is relaxed, reserved and calm, just like Aurora. They are two peas in a pod, no mistaken identity there, like father like daughter. Whilst Raymond will rarely organise a holiday, he will happily tag along, a bit like me and my own voice, it's mutually exclusive.

We took the scenic road on the A6 through Bakewell, Taddington, and Cowdale. I love the names of some of the towns and villages that scatter through the Peak District like, Sparrowpit, Leek, Pikehall and the very amusing name given to the train service in the area: the Glossop Line.

We stopped in Buxton for lunch and what a fine looking little town it was. The main street had been festooned with miles of red, blue, and white bunting (for some sort of festival, which escapes me now). It was eye catching, covering the street in a kind of carnival canopy. There were many people out milling in the cafés and stores, which gave the town a sense of self-esteem. The cobbled streets were clean and there was definitely that sense of pride you find in towns that are prosperous.

Buxton is another 'spa town', not unlike Bath. It too has a long history as a destination for wealthy people to splash around in its geothermal springs as a tonic for well-being. Buxton also has a royal crescent and a pump room, just on a smaller scale.

We parked our car and wandered through the small laneways in search of something to eat.

Lunchtimes on holidays are a bit fraught with danger, you definitely have to compromise about food on holidays but finding something that would please everybody and not break the bank was difficult. Eating lunch out in a restaurant was not really practical with four of us, we tried that and my bank balance felt the pain. £80 for lunch was bit rich and all we had was a fancy sandwich and coffee.

Given the success of the last 'lunch on the go' we decided to try the local supermarket's variety. You could get a pick and mix lunch of a sandwich, drink, and a piece of fruit for less than £5, and there was a lot to choose from, so it covered all bases. A bit of a find when it came to eating on the go. At least we could get a 'healthy option' on a few occasions.

We took our new found lunch deal to the park and sat watching the world go by amongst the swaying daffodil heads.

The Peak District National Park became the first National Park in England in 1951, and it attracts millions of visitors every year. It's strange that it is named the Peak District, because there really aren't any peaks, not in the mountainous, summit kind of way you see in Austria. It was more like a well-rounded curvy hippopotamus bottom, like the drawings my children used to do of hills, all wavy and green, with cows poking out from the sides of them. It was a gorgeous pocket of England, surrounded by large urban areas like Manchester and Sheffield and a lot of those millions of visitors each year came from those surrounding areas. The easy access by car or train, made it so much less cumbersome for people to visit, and the tourists began to come not only for the geothermal spas in Buxton, but the great outdoors as the benefits of spending time in nature became more du jour, especially in the Victorian era.

Buxton had many activities on offer throughout the whole National park; some like paragliding and mountain bike riding were not on our list of must do things. Not even the girls were interested in partaking in anything deemed too energetic.

When Raymond and I were newly arrived visitors to the mother country we got confused a lot. Everyday things were just that little bit different, and while we could speak the language some things just didn't make sense to us at all. I remember seeing an advertisement on the back of a red bus with a child with his teddy bear. The bear's head had fallen off, and the boy had a sad face, with a caption above that read, 'It's time to switch'. I remember thinking what on earth does that mean? Switch? Switch, what? Switch the child for another one? It was apparently an advert for a debit card.

We had many confusing moments in our first few weeks, first class and second class stamps, what was the difference? I still think I probably put the wrong stamped letter in the wrong post box. One of the more confusing aspects was the naming of vegetables. For quite some time I declined the courgette soup because I had no idea what it was, until one day someone told me it was the name for zucchini. I'm glad I didn't order that soup, it didn't sound that appetising after all.

You could also get yourself in a bit of trouble with some of the connotations of words. We use the word thong to describe a particular type of footwear, but the British use flip flop. The word thong in the UK is a G-string (totally different piece of apparel). The word pants in Australia means trousers, and to make it even more confusing, the word pants was British slang for awful. Go figure. It certainly was the cause of misunderstanding and laughter.

I never tire of this hilarious aspect of our two cultures. I was given a British phrase book for a secret Santa gift years ago; I still have it, and it is the source of many giggling sessions. Bollocks is still one of my favourite words.

According to Lonely Planet, "to play on words you need a sense of metaphor, and there's nothing the English language likes more than a metaphor". There are of course thousands of them, and you can apply them to a number of activities—my favourites are from the animal world. Sitting duck, game of cat and mouse, penguin suit, water off a duck's back, and stubborn as a mule. Some are truly hilarious. Our children came across their own causes of fascinating word confusion on this trip.

Apart from not being able to pronounce some of the counties we were driving through (Worcestershire, for instance), and not understanding the names for people from a certain area (Brummies, from Birmingham) they now have quite the additions to their vocabulary. Here are a few:

Knees up, means having a great time (that one was learnt from their godmothers).

Richard the third, is cockney rhyming slang for "turd" which they thought was hilarious. They even learnt an accompanying cockney accent to go with it.

All piss and wind, means all talk and no action, except I am not sure exactly how wee and wind would go together, rather messy I would think?

Words for money (quid), a 'fiver' for £5, a 'tenner' for £10, 'bangers and mash' means cash, and 'a pony' means £25.

Ice Lolly, means flavoured ice on a stick. In Australia those are known as Icy Poles. The girls thought an ice lolly was frozen lollies (which to them sounded disgusting).

And my favourite, sweet fanny, Adams, means you have done nothing all day. That could well explain some of the occasions Aurora and Coco were lying about the house in Sandgate.

CHAPTER 6 – THE LAKE DISTRICT

As we wound our way out of the Peak District we caught the M6 and headed North to the Lake District, and into Grasmere to be exact. It was a few hours driving, and I had put the roof up by this stage as motorway driving was not conducive to having the roof off, and neither was the commentary from the back seat.

The drive was downtime for the girls, time to stick the ear buds in, have a nap, or check their social media. With a few hours to disappear into their 'gadget world', it made for a quiet trip.

The Lake District is the most visited of the National Parks in the UK, and was a lot more mountainous than the Peak District. It is described as the land of "Poets, Peaks, and Pencils". I love that.

The poets being William Wordsworth and Samuel Taylor Coleridge, the Peak being all the mountain tops and pikes in the National Park, and the pencils are reference to Derwent pencils which are still made in the Lake District alongside the Derwent River.

It covers an area of approximately 2,362 square kilometres, and was named as a world heritage site by UNESCO which is pretty impressive. It is located entirely in the English county of Cumbria, and houses the highest mountain in England, Scafell Pike.

As we wound our way onto the A591, with Grasmere on our GPS, we entered the boundary of the Lake District and the first of many lakes came into view.

Lake Windermere is the largest natural lake in England. It is long, skinny and runs for nearly 18 kilometres. It was a clear sunny afternoon and as the sun moved west, the shadows on the lake were cast from the clouds above, making the water seem very dark blue.

We ambled along in Ambleside, and headed up Rydal Road in search of refreshments. It was a very picturesque and attractive Victorian market town, with gorgeous little shopfronts, houses and B&B accommodation. There were agreeable looking shops lining the footpath, from book stores to gift stores, but we were looking for somewhere to have a quick coffee and possibly a piece of cake.

There were a lot of cafés to choose from, and I am not sure what attracted us to the one we went to, but it really wasn't very good.

The service was practically non-existent and it was expensive. It looked great from the outside, and there were people happily sitting out the front, looking like they were enjoying themselves but we were ushered inside and the view out across to the attractive landscape all but disappeared. We ended up ordering drinks only as the kitchen was closed, and the choice of cake looked rather sad and tired on closer inspection. Inside, the décor was slightly tatty and had a 1990's feel about it. The ambience was non-existent, but I didn't let it quell my mood. I was happy we had arrived in this scenic part of the world. We were keen to get to our accommodation for the night as it had been a long day in the car, and without an afternoon pick me up, I was starving.

Back in the late 1990's Raymond and I spent a few weekends in the Lake District because I used to often need to travel to Cumbria for work. I would head up from London on Thursday, and he would join me on Friday night. It was a perfect arrangement.

On one occasion we stayed in Near Sawrey, a small village known mainly for its association with Beatrix Potter. She lived close by at

Hill Top Farm and several of the neighbouring villages were used in her books.

> *It's a gorgeous pocket of Cumbria with whitewashed homes, thatched roofs, and colourful foxgloves in the gardens. In wintertime it is like a scene out of a fairy-tale.*

Our accommodation was an old Georgian home that had been converted into a guest house, and our room was at the very top of the stairs. The door leading into our bedroom must have been designed for Peter Rabbit himself because at 5ft 9", I had to duck my head every time I went through the door. It proved to be even more tricky after a few glasses of red wine.

The restaurant was impeccable. Although I never confirmed it, I am sure the chef had some sort of Michelin star, it wasn't the first time we had happened upon a restaurant in the middle of nowhere that served food of the highest standard.

When we sat down for dinner the chef came to our table and told us they didn't have a menu but he had "cooked up" a few things he thought we might like. The idea was quite unusual to us especially since we were hardly members of the foodie culture but we were blown away by what was served. To this day it is still one of my favourite meals.

The idea of British cuisine was once a bit of joke. This has changed immensely since we lived here back in the nineties. In the years between then and now, the choice of food has improved tenfold. Indian restaurants were the most exotic places to eat in the UK in 1998, now you can have a very decent meal, whatever the budget (although I believe the favourite British restaurant dish is still Chicken Tikka Masala, a dish that doesn't even exist in India).

British cuisine has had somewhat of a revival over the past thirty years. It has gone from plain and boring to world class, I for one am happy about the influx of modern British cooking establishments.

Another memory from our stay was the owner was a massive Rugby Union fan. Unbeknownst to us, Australia was playing England (or Wales or Scotland for all I know) and he was keen to talk tactics with us. He could not possibly have chosen two more inept people; Raymond and I don't know the first thing about Rugby Union. His face dropped when we said we were heading out for the afternoon, I think he thought we would watch the game with him.

We headed to the Derwent Pencil factory (I know, very unexciting, but I happen to love pencils). Derwent pencils are at the top of the tree when it comes to pencils, they are simply the best. As a child, I dreamt of receiving a wooden presentation box filled to the brim with Derwent pencils. That dream never eventuated, so at the age of thirty, I purchased my own. I still have them. They are my pride and joy. Aurora sketches with them from time to time, so I suggested maybe we could take a visit while we were in the neighbourhood. Suffice to say, my children were not as fanatical about pencils as me.

Our accommodation tonight was in Grasmere, a small stone village set on the waters of Lake Grasmere. Our B&B was opposite the walking trail that winds around the lake.

I pulled up in the small car park and admired our surroundings. One side was the majesty of Lake Grasmere, and the other a quaint little building that was over 400 years old. That little building was our accommodation for the night.

Our family room was spacious and it overlooked the lake and its beautiful surrounds. We even had a tiny balcony that really only fitted one person, but all the same it was lovely. The bar next door was named after the main wildlife in the area: the badger. There was apparently a place just near the B&B where badgers come out at night to eat, but we didn't see any which was disappointing.

We decided to have dinner at our B&B, as we were a bit weary and the girls particularly didn't want to travel far for something to eat. The dining room was old fashioned in an exclusive men's club kind of way. It had dark, mahogany coloured wall panelling, an open fireplace, and plush velvet covered dining chairs. The curtains were heavy and although it was still light outside, the light was soft and rosy inside. Aromatic candles were burning on the table and it would be the perfect place for a romantic meal—not necessarily one with your teenage daughters.

I love dinner time conversations with Aurora and Coco, it always surprised me that it was often something small or insignificant that made their day.

Seeing a horse and cart, having a big hot chocolate, stepping inside an old fashioned red telephone box, eating ice cream, picking flowers, and listening to music; everyday things had a newfound meaning when you had the time to just enjoy your surroundings and the company. I was happy, it had been a glorious few days travelling and there was something reassuring about being in this tiny corner of the world.

While I don't advocate drinking in excess, wine makes things just that little bit more relaxed and enjoyable when you are on holidays. Given I was driving most of the time during the day, a lunchtime tipple would not have been in order, but it definitely was at dinner. Some days we drove for several hours, manoeuvring through mountains and plateaus in the rain, booking accommodation en-route and finding suitable places to eat—it was not surprising at the end of the day that I was looking forward to a large glass of wine. It put a smile on my face and made me slouch in my seat with a very satisfying, "Ahh ..."

To be honest, I would have settled for a beer too (and I did) but wine is my favourite and besides, isn't red wine supposed to be good for you?

That night Aurora and Coco had an important TV date. It was Made in Chelsea night. I should explain that my children didn't even know what this reality TV programme was up until a week ago. Jules introduced them to it the night Raymond and I went out for dinner. I cannot believe that show has been on since 2011 and is up to its thirteenth season, I am perplexed as to the attraction of it, but it has quite the following and regularly has over one million people watching it. The mind boggles, really.

Aurora and Coco were hooked after only a few episodes, I on the other hand, thought it was a rather pointless program but that was probably me showing my age.

The girls propped themselves on our queen size bed and positioned the television for maximum viewing. I had to retreat to the one person balcony but I wasn't disappointed in the view. I could have sat looking at the natural wonder for hours... I was also on the lookout for a badger.

As the TV viewing came to a close for the night, we read on social media about the devastating news of a bombing at a concert in Manchester. We had driven through Manchester that very afternoon; how truly shocking and distressing, especially because it was mainly children at the arena where it happened, children the age of my own girls.

It was truly an awful thing to happen. On that sombre note we retired for the night.

~~~

The next morning more sunshine greeted us – phenomenal really – we were expecting the weather to be generally English-like and dreary, but the last two days had been quite the opposite. A brisk walk around the lake was in order, after another full English breakfast it was probably wise to try and walk it off.

It takes about an hour and a half to walk around Lake Grasmere and we knew we wouldn't do the full circuit, but ended up doing about one-third of it. As we made our way down to the walking trail we passed quite a few 'ramblers' off on their morning walks also. That was term I did not know until I lived in the UK, its direct meaning is, "A person who walks in the countryside for pleasure".

Walking is pretty popular in the UK, not just up the High Street to shop but as a recreational activity. It is made quite easy due to a large network of paths, rights of way, and designated tracks for people to walk on, and accessible to everyone. The names given to these outdoor walking pursuits make me giggle. Hiking, hill walking, fell walking, and scrambling, sound more like ingredients for a recipe, than an outdoor leisure activity. In the UK, walking for pleasure really wasn't a thing until the 18th century during the Romantic period; it arose from people's attitudes changing towards the beauty of the surrounding flora and fauna. Up until then, walking was generally associated with poverty and being homeless. Today it is widely recognised that rambling has many health benefits, and going on the amount of organisations that promote the interest of the walker and the maps available... it's actually become a big business.

Today we were simply a family of Australians, soaking in the warm spring air and the fine looking scenery. We certainly were not decked out in outdoor wear like our fellow walkers, but we enjoyed it none the less.

The girls were keen to try out the temperature of the water in the lake, just to see if they could dip their toes in. Several large ducks floated by, followed by their ducklings all straggling behind them flipping about in the water. The girls spied them straight away.

"Look, baby ducks!"

Out came their phones again, taking video and snaps of the furry little creatures. I was really starting to sense a theme here; the girls would go all "aww", whenever we saw animals—especially baby ones. Everyone loves a lamb or a duckling, but I could really see the girls change whenever we encountered an animal. The greyhound at the breakfast table, the baby lambs, and now baby ducks, maybe I should be thinking along a different wavelength when it comes to the activities teenagers want to do? Should I look for zoos, safaris? Anything to keep their interest up.

Our walk around Lake Grasmere was pleasant indeed and as we walked closer to the water's edge, Coco picked up flat stones to skim and climbed the wooden rails that ran alongside the sandy shores.

I don't think you are ever prepared for the sound of a sonic boom. It scared the shit out of Aurora and Coco–they had never heard it before and were not only startled, but looking around for what had made the intense noise above their heads. Obviously the source of the noise had long gone, unless you actually are looking up at the sky before the sonic boom, you will not know it is about to happen. We were fortunate to see the fighter jets circling above ready for another fly by.

I called out to the girls, "Here they come again, listen after they fly past."

It is quite the weirdest thing, a sonic boom. You see the jets flying above but there is no sound, then all of sudden it's like a thousand thunder storms have rained down on you.

On a beautiful clear day in the Lake District it was the last thing

I expected to happen. It is a very unusual occurrence to see military jets flying low over national parks, I cannot think of a place in Australia where it happens (well not one I have visited anyway). It seems to annoy the locals; they are not so keen on their beautiful green space being interrupted with low flying military aircraft, and they had a point. But I guess if the RAF don't do their training exercises in the countryside, where do they do it? Over London?

By far the best part of travel for me, is meeting people. You don't have to be an extrovert to meet people on holidays, it just happens organically. If you really think about the folk you meet, it would add up to the hundreds. The person who makes your coffee, hands you your room key, drives the taxi, serves your food, gives you directions in the street... you may not have a long exchange but you will remember the place and the reason you were there.

I make a habit when I'm on holidays to talk to as many people as I can. I love hearing what other people have to say (except possibly about Rugby Union), it is an insight into humanity, into a life in a foreign country. People always have something to say, conversations can be about the weather, traffic, politics, celebrities, or pets. It doesn't matter what you talk about, it is the interaction with people that gives you insight into this wonderful planet we live on. I am fascinated with the lives people lead, and the everyday things that make a life so interesting and unique. I make a habit of talking to the person sitting next to me on aeroplanes (I know, I am that person you silently wish wouldn't sit next to you), but over the years I have had so many wonderful conversations it restores my faith in human nature.

Travel gives you the opportunity to meet people you would otherwise not come into contact with, it's not about making lifelong friends, but broadening your mind and knowledge of how people live in different countries, communities, and climates. We are so alike in many ways and then so different. Visiting the UK is not dissimilar to life in Australia (except our accents), but life in parts of Europe can be poles apart. There are always common threads; love and family are the big ones.

One of the opening lines in the movie Love Actually is, "If you look for it, I've got a sneaky feeling you'll find that love is actually all around"... and it is. You see it every day, on the streets, in the parks, mothers and babies, fathers and daughters, big families, small families, grandparents, godparents, everyone has that connection. People always want to talk about their families, how proud they are, where they live, their ancestry, these are the stories that fascinate me; I always learn something from these exchanges.

The previous day, I learnt one of the staff at the B&B we were staying at was from a small town in Minnesota (US). He was on an adventure of a lifetime, living and working in the UK on a student visa. He had been there for two days and had no idea how to make a gin and tonic, but I forgave him for that given he would not have been legal drinking age in America. The conversation brought back memories of when my husband and I left the sunny climes of Australia for an English winter. (Our American friend had at least relocated to England for the summer).

Landing in a foreign country is exciting and scary at the same time; I had butterflies as the plane was descending through thick fog into Heathrow airport. I couldn't believe I was actually there, on British soil. I adored the country from the first moment I laid eyes on her. Those first few days made my head whirl, I couldn't believe how beautiful it was, and not just the history, or the ancient buildings, or the rugged landscapes, but the people were so friendly and accommodating to a pair of young antipodeans. I had a fresh perspective on life and an appreciation for this wonderful planet and its inhabitants.

I wished Mr Minnesota his own trip of a lifetime.

In light of the fact we missed Stonehenge, I happened across another "bunch of old rocks" just outside Keswick called Castlerigg. This stone circle was one of around fifty in Cumbria, which made this county a bit of a mecca for stone circles. Won't the girls be happy to know I have found another lot of rocks to see instead of Stonehenge?

Castlerigg has thirty eight stones set in a circle of sorts. They were a bit higgledy piggledy but I guess that was okay, seeing they are estimated to have been built roughly 5,000 years ago. They sat atop a low hill with views across to the neighbouring peaks. No one really knows who built these stone circles or why, and there are many of them in the UK. The main thought is they were used for religious or ceremonial purposes.

On that clear blue day, the stones were quite magnificent and I was very happy the entrance fee was zero. We were nearly the only people there (another bonus) and you could get up close and personal to them because there were no fences. It was a better offering than the other bigger stone circle attractions. It was on a much smaller scale, but equally as impressive, and we had it all to ourselves.

The girls didn't seem that impressed but I spied Coco taking photos while leaning against one of the stones, so it was at least worthy of a photo. She was however very interested in the 'Mister Whippy' ice cream truck stationed just up the side road from Castlerigg. It was a strange addition to the landscape, but I'm sure they do a roaring trade in summer. I however said an ice-cream for morning tea wasn't really that nutritious, even while on holiday... I know, I'm a party pooper.

We were nearing Scotland, and I was getting very excited. I had been looking forward to visiting that magical place for some time. It had been 17 years since we had set foot in Scotland. We celebrated

Hogmanay in Edinburgh in 1999 and saw in the new millennium. It was a once in a lifetime event, and I will always be grateful we not only got to celebrate with tens of thousands of Scots, but with our gorgeous friends from Sandgate.

Scotland is small but it's big on history, architecture, natural wonders, and sassy Scots. I am fond of the beautiful country and its proud people. It has a rich history, too much to go into but I was very much looking forward to exploring the magnificent country and all it had to offer.

When we crossed the border into Scotland I announced it from the driver's seat, the large blue and white St Andrew's Cross was emblazed on the signposts welcoming us to this beautiful land, how exciting!

Unfortunately my passengers didn't share my enthusiasm. The poor weather had started rolling in, and the bottoms of the clouds were drooping towards the top of our car. The dark marbled mass was suspended in the atmosphere above our heads, heavy and full of rain, resembling a heap of inky mashed potato.

CHAPTER 7 – OBAN

Scotland is divided into three areas, the Upper Lowlands, The Central Lowlands, and The Highlands and Islands. The last region covers approximately 50% of Scotland's landmass. There are nearly 800 Scottish islands, with the Shetland Isles being the most northern. We weren't heading that far north but I was excited about heading into the Highlands and experiencing the dramatic scenery I remember from years before… I just hoped that the children would find it as spectacular as I did.

Scotland is quite small, but it packs a lot into its wee area. Each area of Scotland has something very distinct and characteristic of its landscape and people. Its rich heritage is endless.

Some fun facts about Scotland:

The National symbol of Scotland is the thistle. It is purple in colour (as a side note, my sister in law picked one of these from the fields at the bottom of Ben Nevis in 1998 and brought it back to Australia, flattened in her guidebook. She still has it).

Scotland is home to the oldest universities on the world, including the University of St Andrew's, which was founded in 1410.

11% of Scottish people have red hair, which is a higher percentage than in any other country (I like this one… I'm a red head).

The Bank of Scotland is the oldest surviving bank in the UK, founded in 1695.

The modern game of golf originated in Scotland in the 15th century, the golf club, St Andrew's, is widely known as the 'home of golf'.

Shortbread is Scotland's most famous biscuit (particularly good at Christmas when they are in the shape of a Scotty dog!).

Famous Scottish actors include Sean Connery, Ewan McGregor, Billy Connolly, James McAvoy, and Gerard Butler (I think everyone would agree that the Scottish accent is divine).

As we motored up the A76 I saw a sign for a castle. Drumlanrig Castle, in fact. It looked handsome and was only a few miles off the motorway (turned out a longer drive than I originally thought).

As we wound our way through the wavy mounds, it was another landscape altogether. The hill sides were barren of trees and bushes and covered in a dry kind of grass, but it gave the impression of travelling through a slot car set. We were the only car on the perfect roadway intertwining through the rises and drops of the hill crests.

Drumlanrig Castle is imposing when you come around the corner into the estate. It is called the 'pink palace' and I can see why. The exterior is made of pink sandstone and in the late morning sun it had a distinct rosy glow. I have seen many castles in my time, but that one was stunning to look at.

We drove into the grassy car park and headed towards the main gate. Drumlanrig Castle was built between 1684 and 1691—I still cannot get over how old everything here is!—and is now the private residence of the Duke and Duchess of Buccleuch and Queensberry. Wow, I would have loved to live there.

As it happened, the actual castle wasn't open, we had come too early in the year. It predominantly only opens in summer, but the gardens, stable yard, and tea rooms were open, so we headed in the direction of the refreshments first.

We were practically alone in this vast estate bar a few cyclists.

Drumlanrig seems to be a mecca for mountain bike riding, and there were a few adventurers out, but we were the only people visiting.

The castle tea rooms were quaint with many copper kitchenware items stored in shelves along the walls. It had the feeling of a working 1800s kitchen, quite sparse, but rather sweet. We had the whole place to ourselves so of course the service was impeccable. Lunch was a bowl of soup and bread, and an ice cream each as we left. It was simple, but satisfying.

We strolled around the vast gardens (in fact 40 acres worth), and munched on our ice-creams (to make up for the lack of ice cream the day before—okay... yes, I felt bad and relented). I was conscious not to inflict the 'NABC' (not another bloody castle) on the children, it would be easy to see countless castles in the UK and Scotland, there are over 3,000 in Scotland alone. If I suggested seeing even more than a handful there would have been a mutiny in the Mercedes.

As it turned out Drumlanrig was one of only three we visited on our trip, so I think that was quite reasonable.

Unbeknownst to us, when we travelled up the A82 on our way to Oban we drove along the same roads as James Bond in Skyfall (I only found this out afterwards!). We weren't in a sleek Aston Martin, but our Mercedes convertible was pulling the same vibe. There was something special about the landscape, it was utterly stunning. The grey sultry skies, the rugged cliffs and mysterious fog gave me goose bumps. I took a deep breath and gasped at its splendour. On that occasion I did get out of the car and take photos, albeit in the rain. My family thought I was mad, pulling over into the layby to take photos of cliff faces, but I cannot tell you how impressive the valleys, waterfalls and skylines were. No wonder filmmakers use that scenery, it takes your breath away, and as I was standing there, soaking it all in, I started to cry.

I don't know why, I was just overwhelmed with the sheer

splendour of Mother Nature. Our trip through that spectacular countryside was nothing short of perfect.

> *I didn't even care it was raining, I was experiencing first hand natural beauty on a scale I had never known.*

It was mesmerising, I could stand there all day and look at that faultless backdrop. Everyone should experience it at least once in their lifetime.

I had read of a story of a monk who had a special veranda to listen to the rain. This veranda is for the sole purpose of taking time out, and listening and concentrating on the sound of raindrops on the tin roof. "The sound of rain needs no translation," it said.

Being present and listening to your surroundings and soaking in the sheer pleasure of something so simple is splendid. We don't take enough time out of our busy lives to appreciate the very things right in front of our noses. As I stood admiring this remarkable landscape, I truly knew it was one of those moments that can only be described as awe inspiring.

When we experience the emotion of awe we are challenged by the presence of something so much bigger than ourselves. I can totally relate. Standing there amongst this enormous landscape, it makes me feel very small in this very large world. It has been said that this feeling connects us to ourselves and each other.

Thich Nhat Hanh in his book, *'The Art of Living'* talks about time. That there is no such thing as not enough time or too much time– it's your perception. So now (wherever possible) I don't think about time, I just use as many hours in the day as I can, to do the things I love.

It's a great concept. It sums up why I conjure all these travel itineraries and dreams of faraway places to experience with my family. I want the time to enjoy a beautiful sunset, time to hear the birds sing, time to smell the sea air, time to just be. I want to share my memories with my family, and share my love for this amazing world we live in.

"We need to shake ourselves awake so we can change our way of living, so we can have more freedom, more happiness, more vitality, more compassion and more love".

With that thought in mind, I was remarkably upbeat and ready to drive on to Oban, "The seafood capital of Scotland". I had seen glorious photos of the seaside town and my younger sister had visited recently and commented on how lovely it was. I was looking forward to spending a bit of time there and soaking up the Scottish hospitality.

We had booked our accommodation in a small B&B overlooking the Firth of Lorn. As we were making our way along the A85 I noticed a very small railway line, like a Noddy train would glide along there. It was amazing in this mountainous county, with nearly empty roads, to see there was a public transport option. I didn't even know that you could take the train to Oban. Next time I'm in the neighbourhood I will definitely make the journey by train.

The clouds became heavy with rain and started to sink lower in the sky. It was past four o'clock and as we made our way along the shores of Ardmucknish Bay the heavens opened and the heavy plodding raindrops splashed towards the car. The roads glistened with water, and puddles were forming in the potholes. It was no dual lane freeway, and I had to make room for large lorries carrying timber poles to squeeze past on the narrow verges.

As we came down the hill into Oban we could not even see the island of Kerrera, the thick clouds were covering the beauty of the port town, only the twinkle of street lights were visible, guiding us into town like an airport runway. By the time we parked our car at the B&B the weather had really set in, and there was an eerie glow through the rain.

It has often been said that it was 'not about the destination, but the journey'. While spending seven days driving around the UK with family may not be a journey everyone would want to do, I encourage everyone to try it at least once. It can be anywhere. A driving trip to the outback, a snorkelling holiday in Fiji, a walking tour in Spain, a cruise even! Anything to bring you together in a different way than at home.

Prepare yourself to be out of your comfort zone... it's worth it. It's worth getting to truly know your children and your partner. Spending time together in close confines adds another dimension to your family dynamics, it is never what you expect. It is better and worse.

I am guilty of conjuring all these romantic visions of family life, straight out of Ralph Lauren advertisements. I do not deny that I live with my head in the clouds sometimes, but when I'm on holiday it is different. I am different in myself, I am not working, or at school. I don't have those pesky jobs to do around the house, and my days are free of running errands and catching up with correspondence. It is a real chance to just relax and recharge the batteries. As a parent I let my guard down a bit on holidays, but that's when my children really get to see a part of me that isn't so visible at home with the busy lives we lead.

I love seeing the people my children are becoming, they are not little anymore, they are becoming adults and I feel blessed to get to know them. Holidays give you the opportunity to spend time with your family that has no other strings attached; there is absolutely nothing else to do but enjoy each other's company.

Our children started to build an appreciation for us, their Mum and Dad, good timing since they were at the age where we can be embarrassing to them. We get it (and sometimes play on it—my husband has been known to grab their hands and skip down the street) but they have realised we are actually people too. We were young once, seeing that helped them remember they do love us, and maybe we were pretty groovy too. I feel quite chuffed by that.

> *Yes, you grate on each other, that is natural too, but what you gain is an insight to these very special human beings that make you proud, make you cry, make you laugh, make you cranky, and sometimes makes you all of that at the same time.*

The children were quite remarkable in their adaptability, I forget just how easily children adjust to their surroundings, and I worried more than I should. I too suffer sometimes being a helicopter parent, but I try hard to give my children independence and when you are on holiday it is easier to let them go off by themselves and do things on their own. They were generally together, which was great, and it gave them that sense of freedom without being too far away from us.

It was a time I treasure and will never regret. And what better place to be in than Scotland? "A spirit of its own", (according to a recent Visit Scotland advertisement), and I agree, we were having our own spiritual journey.

Family travel was an evolving process, it changed from one day to the next. Raymond and I were seasoned travellers, and we have 'been there, done that' in many of the places we re-visited with Aurora and Coco, which was a completely different beast than travelling as a couple.

It was a big transition time for them (and us): The Teenage Years. I don't think teenagers deserve the bad rap they get, especially when it comes to travelling. They are seen to be negative and difficult, and often have a negative reputation as surly passengers. But I disagree. We should nurture them and understand them during these years, just like any other time. We learn a lot about the society we live in through teenagers. It's a time and a place and yes, they have their moments, of course but it's a grand adventure, a grand tour of life, and as parents we can teach them the philosophy of 'Keep Calm and Carry on' (with a smile on your face!).

Our hosts in Oban were a married couple who were heading off to Inverness the very next day, to celebrate their daughter being married. They were praying the rain would clear for their special family occasion and as I looked out towards the firth, I couldn't see the weather passing anytime soon. It was thick with sea fog, and an eerie twilight glow; I couldn't see two metres in front of me, let alone imagine smiling sunshine wedding weather. But I too, crossed my fingers the weather would improve for our trip in the morning towards the Scottish Highlands.

Our B&B had a mock Tudor feel about it, with white washed walls, black window shutters, and roof tiles. It was built down a hill so the path leading to the reception was down a steep verge to a wooden deck, complete with carriage lamps and handmade wooden chairs. There was a small garden off to the right, with a raised arbour and a bird box, along with a gorgeous hedge of a plant I didn't recognise. I did however recognise the bright purple rhododendrons which sparkled like tinsel from the water droplets.

Big, black tubs of ferns lined the path, and if it hadn't been raining I would have been quite happy to sit there, indulging in a glass of wine and looking out over the firth. Alas, it wasn't the type of weather to be contemplating any outdoor activity.

Our room was spacious and each of our beds had a small teddy bear sitting atop—a cute addition, I thought. Coco especially liked the personal touch to our lodgings for the night (there they go with animals again).

After a few recommendations for dinner, we settled on a quaint little pub just a few streets back from the harbour. There was no view tonight, so it didn't really matter we weren't near the water. It wasn't a fancy pub or a gastropub (although that definition sounds more like you would get sick from eating there!), but it was cosy and on a rainy night, it was perfect. I couldn't believe that at the very next table were two Australians, travelling around Scotland like us. What were the odds? When you are in a small town on the west coast of Scotland, you really don't assume you will run into your own country people.

We chatted about our travels and where we had been, they were at the end of their trip and returning to Australia in the next few days. It was great to hear an Australian accent from someone other than your family. I enjoyed chatting with them, although it was unlikely I would ever see them again—I cannot even remember their names.

The next morning we woke to the same weather pattern we had gone to sleep with the night before. Lots of rain, except it had become very misty.

After breakfast and farewelling our hosts enroute to the wedding, we thought we would explore the town of Oban a bit more than just seeing the inside of a pub. I was disappointed not to see the seaside town in all its glory, considering how amazing it looked on the tourist websites. We only had the day there and the weather wasn't budging at all—in fact it was getting colder and wetter.

The raindrops fell in large dollops and we had to head for cover. We happened across a café that said, "World famous coffee". It seemed like just the place to go to shelter from the rain and have a hot beverage.

I can honestly say it wasn't the best coffee in the world (I still think Melbourne has that honour). It lacked atmosphere, and the seats were hard, but it was a respite from the rain and as it sat on the harbour front we had a view of the ferries coming in and out from the neighbouring islands.

No visit to Scotland is complete without a visit to a scotch malt whisky distillery. The locals call whisky the 'water of life' and it is a true spirit (pardon the pun) of the nation. From one side of Scotland to the other, there are literally thousands of distilleries. I elected for a quick drop-in to the Oban Distillery and took a look around. Given the weather, it was a good choice.

I left the family in the café and turned the corner to the visitors centre. Built in 1794, the Oban distillery was in the middle of the town centre, housed in a very elegant building. It had lovely black bricks encasing the windows, and a five star Scottish tourism award, which hangs proudly at the front door. It was a lovely little distillery, and I did partake in the complimentary "dram" (Scottish for drink), which was rather fine even at 11am.

Apparently during the summer months, Oban can have up to 25,000 visitors, but on that very dreary spring day we were lucky to see 25 people. It was mostly deserted in town. We walked up to the ferry station that takes you across to the neighbouring islands, the Isle of Mull being the closest. I suggested maybe we take a trip there, but was met with downward glances, and, "It looks boring!"

I must admit the weather was a huge deterrent and the thought of being tucked up inside our warm car was a better option. After only an hour in the Oban town centre, we drove north up the hill and out towards the Scottish Highlands.

CHAPTER 8 – THE SCOTTISH HIGHLANDS

When we visited Scotland in 1998, my sister in law wanted to do the rather energetic walk up the tallest mountain in Scotland, Ben Nevis. Raymond and I weren't that keen as it was an eight hour round trip, but we were very happy for her to do it.

I was so sure we waved her off on her walk from the town of Fort William, but when we got there, it didn't look familiar. I had very fond memories of the day she climbed Ben Nevis, it was a flawless sunny September day, the picturesque town at the foothills was perfect, and I distinctly remember the cashmere and wool stores, and the pub (I'm sure there were other shops there but I cannot remember). I had a vision in my mind, but as we approached Fort William, I did not recognise anything. Was I thinking of somewhere else?

We parked our car near a toilet block and headed to the high street which is pedestrianised. It had stopped raining, but the wind was picking up and it was terribly grey and dull. We looked for a place to eat and walked up and down the cobbled high street to no avail, all the eating establishments were a bit grim looking and the pub, whilst lovely looking on the outside, had a very unpleasant odour once we walked in. We high-tailed it out of there before the smell got too stuck in our nostrils.

We eventually found a café with plump sofas in the front

windows and a very small menu. Our lunch consisted of coffee and chocolate cake, which wasn't on the healthy eating scale but was somewhat adequate.

We took a look around, on the hunt for a few gifts. I am not a huge souvenir purchaser, but I did want to get some small Scottish gifts for friends and family. Something made in Scotland, and small enough for me to carry home to Australia. I happened across a fantastic little store called "The Highland Soap Co.", which makes handmade soaps and natural skin care products. It was lovely and the staff were helpful and informative. I carried several bags out of there, happy I had made all my gift purchases in one shop, job done. Apart from that rather delightful find, there was nothing else in Fort William we wanted to hang around for. I was convinced it wasn't the place I had remembered from years ago.

When we got back to the car, I grabbed out the map and looked for towns in the vicinity that might jog my memory. The name Glencoe seemed familiar and seeing we were on route to Crieff to visit family, Glencoe was (kind of) on the way. With much enthusiasm I said, "Let's head to Glencoe."

Aurora and Coco weren't that fussed really, they were happy to get out of the blustery weather. I had read Glencoe was one of the many locations in Scotland for the Harry Potter movies. Apparently the third instalment of the movie had been filmed there, so that was an incentive for Coco to head south again.

Glencoe is Scotland's most famous glen, with a dramatic backdrop of breathtaking peaks and waterfalls. The name means 'narrow glen' and it was formed by volcanic activity followed by glacial erosion, which subsequently formed the steep sided mountains seen today.

As we approached Glencoe, I really didn't recognise anything there either. The afternoon was getting along by this stage, and we still had to drive to Creiff for our family engagement, so we couldn't stop long. We did an illegal U-turn and headed south along the A82. I was disappointed I didn't get to see the gorgeous little town of my memories, but what I didn't realise was the road we were heading down is the most magnificent drive in Scotland.

Heading across Glencoe mountain and through the ski resorts (not the time of year for skiing, but you could see how spectacular it must be in winter), the road meanders up and over the hillocks, mountains, and plateaus. It is vast and breathtaking. The vegetation changes rapidly from heather covered hillsides, to rocky outcrops, to flat plains with a distinct orange foliage. I had no idea what species it was, but its vibrant colour was arresting. It was like a shagpile carpet from the 70s, thick, plush, with hues of ginger. It had to be one of the top ten drives in the world, even in the misty rain it was nothing short of dramatic and grand on a scale I had never seen before. This was Mother Nature at her best.

It has often been said we shouldn't recreate holidays, we should remember the holiday for the memories created previously, because if you do the exact same holiday again, you will be disappointed. I'm afraid I do not agree. I have recreated holidays and each time they have been just that little bit different, you can never have exactly the same experiences anyway, and that's the best part. It's familiar but new, all at the same time. We were creating a whole set of different memories.

As a child, Raymond used to go to the same holiday house on the NSW Central Coast for nearly eighteen years. Every school holidays, every summer break, was spent in the same place. He loved it and has very fond memories; it was a place in time, a place of his childhood. Every time he visited it was different, it may have been the same place, the same beach, the same neighbourhood, the same people, but each time there was something special about being there. It was about family and spending time together, La Famiglia, that's what our holiday was about too.

On our tour in 1998 we headed north to Inverness, the area mainly known for the Loch Ness Monster. Aurora and Coco were keen to visit that part of the Highlands, but we couldn't fit it into the schedule. They were disappointed, it was one place they did want to go. But it was a two hour drive along the shores of Loch Lochy to Loch Ness, which would have been an incredible sight, but alas, it was too far.

Inverness is renowned for historic attractions, natural wonders, and of course the legend of the sea monster affectionately known as Nessie. My husband, sister in law, and I, spent a few days in the legendary spot. The myth surrounding Nessie is fabled. It was one of the world's top ten mythical creatures, up there with trolls and yetis. There have been up to 1,000 recorded sightings of Nessie, and there is actually an official Loch Ness Monster Fan club. I particularly like the fun fact that the Thatcher government seriously considered an official "Loch Ness Monster Hunt".

On our 1998 visit to Loch Ness we visited the obligatory visitor centres, which from memory were actually quite good. Lots of grainy film footage, the famous photo, and Nessie inspired tourist tat. The most memorable part of the visit was where we stayed the night.

In 1998, we had to consult a travel guidebook and depending on the date of publication, the information could either be totally up to date or obsolete. Happily the B&B we chose was still in business when we made the call from a telephone box (I know, do they still exist?). When we arrived we were met at the front door by the owner who was very happy to see us, but profusely apologetic for the fact that they were in the middle of redcurrant picking season. I had no idea what that meant, but as we entered the kitchen, I got the gist of it. The kitchen table was piled high with hundreds of wooden trusses with little red fruit dangling like little Christmas decorations. They were picked by hand. Redcurrants bare their fruit on old wood; they look by all intents and purposes dead, but with firm and juicy berries hanging off them. I was mesmerised, how delightfully charming and old worldly. I can see that kitchen scene as clearly today, as I saw it then.

In Scotland, redcurrants are mainly used for sauces and jellies, but apparently you can even make whisky out of them (when I buy my Scottish made redcurrant jelly now, I secretly hope the berries have been picked from the same kitchen).

As we followed the A85 towards Creiff, we passed tiny little villages (the blink and you miss them variety) and passed a very splendid Loch called Loch Earn, along with the gorgeous town of Lochearnhead. The tiny little locality is picture perfect. It laps the loch and is edged by a magnificent mountain backdrop. Even on a rainy afternoon, it was a heavenly view. Winding our way around the edges of the loch was spellbinding, each corner was another postcard landscape. The road was quiet and we had the view all to ourselves.

On the south west corner of the loch was the remains of a crannog (an ancient dwelling constructed in a lake) and has been there since the Iron Age. I find these little lodgings most intriguing. Many Scottish lochs are littered with crannogs, they are in all states of disrepair but some are remarkably intact (albeit underwater). They were predominantly thatched, timber roundhouses that were supported on wooden poles driven into the bed of the loch. Looking at them today, they look oddly like our modern day piers we have at the seaside, and the tops look like huts you would find in tropical climes like Bali, thatched and looking like a dunces cap.

Like a moat, the surrounding waters were the inhabitants defence against intruders. I am not quite sure what they would have done seeing people coming across the loch towards their home, but at least they had warning. It must have been rather inconvenient to live in a crannog, it wasn't like you could just duck out for a quick coffee, you would have had to haul a boat across to the shore and if you had too much to bring back it would have meant several trips.

They're so common, there is even a 'Scottish Crannog Centre', a whole centre dedicated to those peculiar little houses. It is located on Loch Tay which was a bit too north for us, but how brilliant that a place has reconstructed one of the ancient dwellings. You can visit it and pretend you lived thousands of years ago.

CHAPTER 9 – CRIEFF

Crieff was an unexpected delight, not only because we were visiting family, but what a gorgeous little market town it is. Crieff sits on the southern edge of the Scottish Highlands with a population of almost 6,000 people.

A fun fact: actor Ewan McGregor grew up there, and he stopped via Crieff on his way to Cape Town in South Africa on his motorcycle tour 'Long way down' with Charley Boorman. (I thought I had seen the town centre before somewhere). It was like we were retracing their tracks (albeit on four wheels), but not going anywhere near as far as South Africa... although our Mercedes would have easily been up for the challenge.

We arrived in the late afternoon and had booked ourselves into a fancy hotel, we figured at least one of the nights we should soak up some luxury. The hotel was originally a Victorian Baronial house and it sat atop a hill behind the town of Creiff. The views over the Perthshire hills and the surrounding woodlands were spectacular.

The weather had thankfully started clearing as we wound our way out of the Highlands and although still cloudy, the rain had stopped, and trickles of light were coming through the clouds. In the late afternoon glow, the hotel was casting splendid shadows as we drove up to the reception.

The grand staircase leading to the front door was guarded by two stone lions, and at the front of the hotel was a turret of sorts, similar to what you see in Disney castles with chimney pots behind. All so medieval looking.

The interior didn't disappoint either, a beautiful stained glass window sat behind a very grand wooden staircase, and dotted throughout were many reminders of the fact we were in Scotland.

We had a few hours to kill before meeting our family for dinner, and Aurora spied the in-house 'Spa' sign. The girls pleaded for a restorative massage to iron out the kinks after sitting in the back seat of the cramped Mercedes all afternoon. I agreed they could have a few hours of pampering and made a booking for them both. My husband retreated to the indoor pool, whilst I decided to put my walking shoes on and hit the pavement.

The late afternoon became quite sunny and I headed off down the hill towards the town centre in search of the perfect gift to take to my family's house that evening. I am a fan of just meandering, of walking the streets in suburbs where people reside, and taking a peek over their fences, imagining what sort of family lived behind them.

The gorgeous little streets zig-zagged down the hill and I was day dreaming about what it would be like to live there. I just love these little corners of the earth, tucked away and almost secret, but all so very normal at the same time.

As a tourist, I am fascinated by how people live in different countries of the world. I have traversed many cities, town, and villages, and while the buildings are different, the landscapes unique, the language distinctive, they all have one thing in common: family.

We may not be able to choose our family, but we still love them. They are our ancestry, the past, the present, and the future.

"Having somewhere to go is home.
Having someone to love is family.
Having both is a blessing."
– Unknown

    I do believe a home is where the heart is, and I saw hundreds of them that day, there was a real sense of community there. With that thought, I got spring in my step, which was just as well as I had to climb back up the steep hill to the hotel.

Catching up with family is always a blessing especially when you live on the other side of the world. We chatted, exchanged stories, asked each other questions about how our families entwined, and generally had a laugh along with a few glasses of wine.

    We had strong family genes. I felt an instant connection with my cousin and her children, like I had known her all my life, strange isn't it? Genetics. I couldn't believe how alike we were even though we had grown up in different countries.

    My cousin said, "I love having all of these lovely cousins in Australia related to me through Nana, who I loved so much. It makes me feel like I have yet another connection with her."

    I cried.

We then headed down to the town centre for dinner at a trendy little restaurant with polished wooden floors. There was a neat set of white windows at the front and topiaries at the door. It was a mild night, and the front door was left open for a cooling breeze.

    Aurora and Coco were happy to sit outside and spend some time away from the gown ups gas-bagging about family trees and ancestry. It was "boring" as they put it. One day I hope they remember meeting all their relatives, and understand the importance of their family heritage. At their age though, it was more important to check their social media.

We had to take the girls out of school for a number of weeks to do the trip and whilst we didn't encounter any backlash from their school, swapping school for travel it is not encouraged, especially for long periods. It's the Traditional Classroom vs University of Life. I like that saying, because it really sums up how I feel. It has been said that what children gain from travelling, far outweighs anything they could learn in the classroom for those few weeks... and I agree.

> *Being a parent is one of the hardest jobs you will ever do and there is no university course for it. You muddle along in blind terror most of the time, but somehow you survive.*

As I looked out across the street, I amazed myself at just how well adjusted our children were. Was it good luck, or had we done a better job than we thought? Who would ever know?

The girls were spinning around a lamp post, giggling to each other, and pretending it was a maypole. Sometimes they were grown up, sometimes they were childish, depending on the moment. It brought a smile to my face.

Travelling has given me the chance to see life through a new perspective, and for my children to see their lives differently too. It is easy to be caught up in the dramas that present themselves to us during our day to day life. Taking yourself out of normality is like a breath of fresh air, there is no schedule, and it doesn't matter what day it is. There is something very liberating about not caring about anything, just taking in every moment of the day, seeing the sun rise, listening to the rain, smelling the sea air, living in the now. It is a skill to be able to stop in this busy world of ours, and just stand still and take in your surroundings. I want to teach the children that, teach them to take notice, talk to people, be out of your comfort zone, experience life through a new aspect. We don't always get that chance at home, but I had the chance now.

The perfect thing about travelling to a new country, a new place, or a new culture is the way it changes how you think about something or someone. There are no other cares or hassles like in your regular life. I really grew up the first time I left Australian shores. Travel made me more independent, confident, and less anxious than I had ever been. I had to stand on my own two feet, I had no choice. I am a better person for it today. If I was going to be the best parent I could be, then I needed to teach them about finding their own self-defining journey, to open their minds to the possibility of seeing their lives through a new lens.

I looked forward to hearing how they thought their perspective had changed after the trip. It was the university of life, the greatest gift we can give our children.

Learning while you travel is an unexpected joy, my children were doing it everyday on that trip, and I suspect they didn't always know we snuck in those little tidbits of information. But when they recall something later, I'll feel a sense of accomplishment that the trip wasn't in vain. I asked them questions along the way (just in case they did forget why we were there). "Why is this place a big deal?" Which was super helpful when trying to explain why we were looking at churches and castles.

At that point, I'd learnt to put a 'child' spin on it. "Did you know the Duke of Atholl has his own private army at Blair Castle? Rumour has it he has a secret underground lair, a shark tank, and white cat?" (The rumours were grossly untrue apparently, but helpful when you need a few moments to yourself while your children search for an allusive cat).

Perthshire spreads into the mountains and makes you feel

instantly at home and welcome. The area feels like the heartland of Scotland, there are plenty of trips looping through the grand glens of the central Highlands and there is wonderful sense of space and openness. It had the impression nothing had ever changed there, like it was almost timeless. The country is so unspoilt, looking at the spectacular countryside, which only changes with the seasons and the cloud formations. It feels like the "real" Scotland.

The hotel was unexpectedly quiet, it was mid-week, so I expect it came to life on the weekends. The hotel advertised it was an ideal location for weddings, and I could see how magical it would be to have a winter wedding there. Imagine all those snow covered turrets, and the warmth of the raging fireplaces inside.

Winter is my favourite time of the year, my family do not share my preferred season (as I have mentioned before), but there I was imagining Christmas in the snow in Scotland. I dared not suggest such a holiday, it was hard enough convincing everyone to travel in Spring.

It seems to be a world over phenomenon to talk about the weather, in the UK it was not just a pastime, it was almost like a religion. You could talk to someone for hours about the weather. Most of the conversations we had with the people we encountered started along the lines of, "Looks like you may need an umbrella today", or, "It's going to be a hot one".

The next few days in Scotland were going to be warm, up to 28°C, and that is what Scotland calls a heatwave! You become quite immune to hot weather growing up in Australia. 28 degrees is not a heatwave in Australia, 42°C is. So we were buoyed by the prospect of having some really pleasant sun drenched spring weather.

Sparkling sunshine puts you in the best of moods and we were all very much looking forward to setting out towards Edinburgh.

CHAPTER 10 – EDINBURGH

Raymond and I had visited Edinburgh twice, and both times I fell in love with the capital city of Scotland, it is a city to remember. Edinburgh is home to fascinating history, beautiful architecture, gorgeous parks and gardens, and of course high-spirited Scots... and not just because it is the home of whisky. It has the whole package – there is something for everyone and given there were four of us all wanting to do varied things on our trip, we had the perfect place now to keep everyone happy.

Before we could do anything it was imperative to find a laundromat. Very pedestrian and not glamorous, but dirty clothes were not high on our wish list so they had to be laundered. It was the humdrum part of travel, the part that has to be done regardless, unless you were prepared to buy new clothes every second day, it had to be factored into the itinerary.

Raymond volunteered to be the chauffeur of dirty linen and proceeded to find a laundromat close by. It proved difficult, as it turns out there aren't many laundromats in Edinburgh. Search cafés, bars, even chimney sweeps, and you will find dozens more than a place to wash your clothes. He ended up having to head back out of town on the outskirts of Edinburgh to find one. He dropped us off in the Haymarket on the way, and resigned himself to spending the morning watching our clothes spinning around.

Thankfully he managed to find a coffee shop nearby and retreated there whilst awaiting the inconvenience of dirty clothes.

Aurora, Coco and I headed up towards Princes Street in the city centre. I had agreed they could do some shopping (I had to eventually), this part of Edinburgh is called the 'New Town' and it houses the chain stores and souvenir shops. Behind it was George Street, which is the location of the more chic and exclusive stores, especially the jewellery stores the girls were interested in visiting.

Our first stop was a sports store, not what I had thought from the outset, but they were both keen to get a new pair of runners each (it boggles my mind they felt the need to have more than one pair). Of course they had to be 'brand' name so I left them inside perusing the myriad of options, whilst I headed across the road to the Princes Street Gardens. The extensive ribbon of green divides Edinburgh in two and as I stood on the path, I took in all the splendour of glorious Edinburgh Castle. It dominated the skyline, the historical fortress cannot be missed, and it was the most recognisable symbol of Edinburgh. As a royal castle, it had been the residence of Scotland's kings and queens, and every occupant had added to the original structure so it's become a wonderful mix of palace, fortress, chapel and war memorial.

Edinburgh Castle is also home to the Scottish Crown Jewels, the oldest regalia in Britain. Displayed with the crown jewels is the Stone of Destiny, returned to Scotland after 700 years in England, where it had sat beneath the Coronation Chair in Westminster Abbey. The stone has an interesting history, for what looked like a big lump of rock.

The castle was on the other side of the park and called the 'Old Town' (easy to see why). Located at the bottom of the Royal Mile is the Holyrood Palace which is the official residence of Queen Elizabeth II. The Royal Mile is a succession of cobblestoned and paved streets forming the main thoroughfare of the old town. As the name suggests, it is a mile long (a 'scots' mile, which is longer than an English mile).

Given I had told the girls they could do some shopping, the deal was that I got to explore the Old Town too. I ventured back inside the sports store to find them and was immediately hit by how warm it was inside. I quickly realised the store was not geared up for hot weather.

It was pretty much the case for every store we went into thereafter. I guessed they would have far more cold days than hot in Scotland so heating would have been imperative but air conditioning was something they most likely never used. So why bother about the expense of putting in cooling?

I would have welcomed it, that was for sure. I was sweating profusely and as a menopausal forty-something woman, it was uncomfortable at best. I couldn't get out of there quick enough. I handed over a £50 pound note to each of the girls and said, "I'll meet you in the shade around the corner". I was starting to sound very un-Australian.

The girls finally appeared with shopping bags and whilst I was pleased they found what they were looking for, the expedition in the sports store was close to an hour long and was only the first store we visited. It was looking less likely I would have time to venture for too long around the parts of Edinburgh that fascinated me. The thought of traversing around shops for the next four hours was akin to stabbing myself in the eye.

I know (most) teenage girls love shopping, my children were of that breed certainly, and if they found 'you can only buy it overseas', then all the better. Granted there were stores in the UK we didn't have in Australia, and as far as bragging rights go, it was a no brainer to shop in those exclusive establishments. It was fair to let them spend their time (and my money!) enjoying the activities they wanted to do. I accepted it wasn't just a holiday to see scenery and old buildings (albeit spectacular), a family holiday should be about everyone. I resigned myself to the fact I would be spending the foreseeable future loitering outside fashion stores. That was okay as the view was definitely better than average.

As I stood on the broad pavement of Princes Street my mind wandered back to 1999. I had stood in the exact same spot 18 years ago for Edinburghs Hogmanay Millennium celebration. The slogan was ehy2k, the time of your life. I remember the time like it was yesterday. We had travelled to Edinburgh by train just after Christmas from London with Jules and Kate (yes, the ones from Sandgate) and we were all very excited. Edinburgh put on quite a show that time of year but that year was different—we were seeing in a new century. There were city wide celebrations, from festive lights, huge Christmas trees, torchlight processions, to winter wonderlands, ice skating and a carousel. There were a huge number of events and most of them were free. In 1999 Hogmanay was a seven day celebration. We couldn't think of a better place to be celebrating the passing of one millennium into the next. We had pre-paid for our street party tickets and bought YEAR 2000 tiaras ready for the celebrations.

As the clock struck twelve midnight, the fireworks erupted from the back of Edinburgh castle and we were showered with pyrotechnic shooting stars and blazing light. It was the best firework display I had ever seen. We had the time of our lives and revelled into the wee hours of January 1 and sang Prince's song 1999 until our voices were hoarse. It is memory I will have forever.

Visiting a new city is a curious and introspective experience. It is an assault on all your senses, new sounds, smells, sights.

Think about whenever you have visited a place for the first time, how did you feel? It is possibly the best feeling in the world, it is never what you expect.

Before you travel anywhere, it almost seems obligatory to ask someone who has previously visited the place for their viewpoint, hints, and tips. Even the advice of a guidebook.

I had been guilty in the past of reading far too much into the opinions of others and had unrealistic expectations of what to expect. I think we all do this at some point, not just in relation to travelling. No travel experience is ever truly dreadful, there are lessons in all experiences, even if it means you will never do it again (I especially feel that way about riding a camel).

We have to trust our own judgement when we travel, trust we can be our own explorer, our own passenger on our own pilgrimage of self-discovery and education. Asking yourself questions and being curious of your surroundings is thoughtful and contemplative. It's a skill we rarely use in this busy world of ours. This trip gave us all the chance to trust that inner part of ourselves. Experiencing something for the first time is enlightening and life affirming. I wanted us all to have that education

We finally made our way across the Princess Street gardens, past the Scott Monument, which is spectacular and an easy to see landmark. This famous structure can be climbed by a staircase of 287 steps, not something we intended on doing, given the weather.

It was past midday and the lawns were becoming the place to be for the lunchtime crowd. On that unseasonably warm Scottish day, the crowds flocked to the gardens in search of a sunny position to soak up the sun's rays. I expected some of them ended up with a case of mild sunburn; there was a lot of pale skin on show. We huffed and puffed up the mound towards the castle, and the street was practically vertical. But it was worth it for the view back towards the gardens and Waverly Street Station. It was busy up there, the pavements were bustling, if you closed your eyes you could just imagine what it would have been like in the Middle Ages, lots of noise and clatter. There was also the very distinct sound of bagpipes.

I hadn't heard them once since we arrived in Scotland and depending on your view, that could have been a blessing but I happen to like the sound. I remember as a child listening to Mull of Kintyre by Wings, the bagpipe part is one of my favourites and who can go past ACDC's Long way to the top? That bagpipe solo is the business. There on the Royal Mile was a young Scotsman dressed in his kilt, bear skin hat and white coat, belting out tunes for the masses on the street. I cannot imagine how hot he must have been in all that attire on the abnormally warm day. He had a small tin positioned in front of him for gratuities and I threw a few gold coins in because I thought the poor thing must have been frying on the inside.

Edinburgh Castle is the backdrop to one of the most famous performances, the Military Tattoo. The royal Edinburgh Military Tattoo takes place once a year in August. It is a parade of bagpipes, drums, and the Scottish regiment. It also includes performers from all over the world. I remember watching this spectacle on television when I was a child; it now attracts an annual broadcast audience up to 100 million people. I have never seen it in real life, but I believe it is awesome.

The type of shopping on the Royal Mile is more Scottish souvenirs than Princes Street and does not contain any chain stores or many cafés for that matter.

I was in desperate need of a coffee and the girls where getting hungry by that stage. We ended up having lunch much further down on North Bridge. We found some fabulous little stores that sold tartan scarves, Scotch whisky and Gin– all the things I wanted to buy. The children picked a couple of very handsome looking scarves for themselves (we were going home to winter in Australia, after all), and I picked up a bottle of local gin for Jules.

Lunch sort of turned into dinner because by that stage Raymond had joined us and we were very keen to soak up the balmy evening air and just watch the world go by. How lovely it was. It was special to not only be in that wondrous city but the weather had really turned on the glory. The added bonus of twilight gave us hours of well-lit scenery and people watching. I could have sat there all night.

The crowds were out in force, all soaking up the extra Vitamin D, just like us. The atmosphere was so joyous, everyone had a smile on their face, it is amazing what sunshine could do. There was no better place to be at that moment, it was splendid indeed.

Another delightful feature in Edinburgh was they had black cabs, just like London. I absolutely love black cabs. Their bubble shape, inward facing doors, spacious 'Tardis' like interior, and rumbling engine were so unique, and even better, you could always guarantee you would get a lively conversation from the driver.

I have never had a black cab ride I didn't like. We hadn't had a black cab trip so far so I announced to the family we were taking that mode of transport. It was as magical as I remember. I likened it to being like a magic carpet ride (if they existed).

We booked our accommodation in Edinburgh a few nights before, and there really wasn't much to choose from. It was a busy time there and we had left our run a bit late. We eventually found a B&B just a few kilometres from the Haymarket. It wasn't flash, but our hosts were absolutely delightful in a slightly bogan fashion that I adored.

They were a husband and wife team, and there were three bedrooms available for overnight accommodation. We only needed one (but in retrospect, we could have done with the second bedroom), so we opted for the family room that looked out over the street of near identical houses. It was very sweet, tidy, and decorated tastefully. It wasn't that big, but we settled into our cramped quarters okay.

Aurora and Coco had a bunk bed and Raymond and I had the double bed. There was a very small bathroom that had been just sectioned off and a wet area added, it wasn't the best conversion I have ever seen but for one night, it was manageable.

It was a warm, humid night and we had all the windows open, propped up with books as the pulley system wasn't working. I was still amazed at how nowhere in the UK had fly screens, I guess because there wasn't anything flying around. If I left my windows bare at home, I would have had an army of mosquitoes descending on us within seconds.

There was something quite reassuring about the low hum of traffic, and the far away voices drifting upwards to our room. It was familiar and peaceful. Coming from a big city, we were used to the murmur of noise, unlike our last few nights' accommodation, which were largely silent. That night I slept soundly, with the balmy night air moving over my face.

The next morning we made our way downstairs to the breakfast part of our B&B and were astounded at the amount of food laid out in front of us. We looked around to see if anyone else was arriving but alas no, it was just us. I had never seen so much food for four people.

Our host appeared from the kitchen in her fluffy purple dressing gown and proceeded to tell us what was on offer for breakfast, there was more! I think I gasped at that point, there was already enough there to feed a small village. She had also prepared a hot breakfast of bacon, eggs, square sausage, haggis, mushrooms, and tomato, all on top of the pastries, yoghurt, pancakes, fruit, muesli and scones.

She clearly thought we hadn't eaten for a week. It was most

generous of her to prepare all that food for us, but there was no way we could eat it all, not even if we stayed another week. She was by far my favourite person I encountered in Scotland. She talked non-stop, smoked in the kitchen, fed the dog from the floor in front of us, and cackled at her own jokes. She was hilarious, she was one of a kind and I am so glad we met her... and, no, I didn't eat the haggis.

CHAPTER 11 – ALNWICK

We were on the downhill run of our road trip (literally, we were heading back into England) and on our way to the historic city of Durham, via Alnwick. It was quite a pleasant drive from Edinburgh because you essentially followed the coastline overlooking the North Sea. Alnwick is a market town in Northumberland and it has been around since 600 AD. It changed very little in that time and was the quaintest English village I had ever seen. Little higgledy piggledy shops lined the high street, interspersed with rows of houses whose front doors were practically on the street.

We wandered around the streets in the search of caffeine (for me) and marvelled at the architecture. Smack bang in the middle of the road was a tower with a hole underneath it to let traffic through.

The main attraction there was Alnwick Castle and as you walked around the corner off the high street, you could not miss it. It was the home of the Duke of Northumberland and is quite famous because it had been used as the exterior and interior of Hogwarts in the Harry Potter films. That was the main reason we headed there, Coco is a huge Harry Potter fan, and seeing the castle in real life was well worth the visit.

We picked a good day to go, it was rather quiet and we had large parts of the property to ourselves. The castle was recorded as having more than 800,000 visitors a year, so I was glad there were much less than that there. As we stood admiring the majesty of the castle, it was hard to believe a family lived there. Part of the castle was open to the public and showed the family living areas. I was surprised to see it was just like any other household, photos on the sideboard (including pets), books, lived in furniture and pot plants. It all looked very normal–if you didn't look outside at the scale of the place.

The weather was continuing to be glorious and wandering around the castle grounds was very agreeable. There were quite a few different activities available on the castle grounds like broomstick training, knights' quests and dragon quests. I was enthusiastic about the broomstick training but was met with rolled eyes from my teenagers.

"It will be fun," I said.

"Well why don't you do it then, Mum?"

Salty! (The new slang I learnt on holiday, which means irritated or angry). I thought the Harry Potter inspired activity would be a winner but evidently not. Too cool for school. So we sat on the grass and watched everyone else do the broomstick training, and it definitely looked like fun. Pity the broomsticks didn't actually fly—now that would be something.

Selfie. Now there's another word that didn't exist in 1998. My children love a selfie. I on the other hand, cannot get the angle correct and end up taking a photo of my eyebrow. I am not practised at it and clearly I need to spend time reading the, "Taking a selfie 101".

So why is it that kids will take endless selfies of themselves, but when you want them to have their picture taken as a family for our photo book souvenir they duck down, hide away, cover their faces and generally have a stroppy expression?

Answer me that... I suspect they didn't want their photo taken with Mum and Dad. We got home from our big holiday with barely a photo of the four of us.

Another interesting note (or alarming, depending on your view) was my husband had taken to posing in our family photos like Derek from Zoolander. He was perfecting the 'blue steel' look, and I am not sure looking back on the photos whether to laugh or cry. They do look rather odd. I guess it was a 'had to be there' moment.

So my family snapshots of the trip were Raymond pursing his lips and staring down the camera like a crazed person, Aurora wearing sunglasses, Coco pulling a face, and me trying to get everyone to say cheese. I could hardly hang that above the fireplace.

In medieval times there were three parks that surrounded Alnwich Castle to the north, west, and south, but Hulne Park is the only one that survived.

Hulne Park was transformed in the 18th century with the aid of our friend from Bath, Lancelot "Capability" Brown. Another interesting garden at Alnwick was the Poison Garden–home to some of the most deadly plants in the world. There were skulls and crossbones on the gate, and you need a guide to take you through, and well worth the visit. If you have never seen a marijuana plant in real life then that is the place to see it.

We continued on the A1 towards Durham past the 'Angel of the North'. You cannot miss her, she towers over the motorway. She is 20 metres tall and her wingspan is 54 metres. It is a steel sculpture that was built in 1998 and it cost £800,000, which was funded by the National Lottery. That wasn't the first time that we learnt the National Lottery had paid for restoration work, arts, and culture; I think it is really quite exceptional.

Fun facts. The following major tourist attractions have been partly, or wholly, funded by the National Lottery:

Tate Modern (and it's free to get in).
Somerset House (great in Winter with the ice skating rink).
The Millennium Bridge (yes, the wobbly one!).
National Portrait Gallery.
Southwark Cathedral.
(And the list goes on).

When Raymond and I first arrived in London in 1997, there was a television show solely dedicated to the national lottery draw. The show went for an hour and attracted some very famous singers, actors, and musicians. It was the highlight of Saturday night TV. We thought it quite strange the time slot had been totally dedicated to numbered balls being drawn from a barrel.

We had nothing like that in Australia, nor Noel Edmonds House Party, which aired afterwards. Noel Edmonds was, from memory, filmed in a large house in a made up village called Crinkley Bottom, and consisted of funny skits and famous guests. On a cold winter's night, it was perfect television viewing. I was quite captivated by television when we first moved to the UK and I thought it was marvellous you didn't have to watch advertisements on the BBC. You paid a fee not to watch ads—I liked it a lot.

CHAPTER 12 – DURHAM

In our four and half year stay in the UK, we had never visited Durham, and I must say it was worth the stopover.

It was a glorious spring afternoon when we arrived and as we approached Durham city, the majestic Durham Cathedral came into view. I was looking forward to seeing the UNESCO World Heritage site, along with Durham Castle.

As a side note, Durham Cathedral is also another film location for Harry Potter. The Cathedral's ancient cloisters double for Hogwarts in the 2001 film Harry Potter and the Philosophers Stone. The cloisters became the snow covered quadrangle where Harry released his owl Hedwig. I could see why filmmakers chose that magnificent building, it was inspiring just to look at, let alone learn all the rich history. Built in 1093, it was a place of worship for almost a millennium. I was very keen to take a peek inside.

Aurora, Coco and Raymond decided they would try out the pool at the hotel. It was an unexpected luxury as we hadn't realised our night's accommodation had a large pool downstairs, and they were keen to soak up some of those sunbeams and splash around in the cooling water.

It was a lovely walk through the market place and up Saddler Street with its little higgledy piggledy shops and restaurants. Durham is quite hilly and I was breathing heavily when I spied a place that looked excellent for dinner. I popped my head in the door and booked a river side table for four, and they were so accommodating and friendly. We had a table right on the outside balcony, overlooking the River Wear, an amazing spot amongst the trees high up on the hill. I actually thought it was a book shop when I first saw the façade, it had that olde world look about it, and given the academic history of Durham, I assumed such a fine looking building would be something to do with education.

Durham is home to Durham University, which is claimed to be England's third oldest after Oxford and Cambridge. It was easy to tell it is a University town because there were a lot of young people there. I really liked that–it gave the town a sense of vibrancy, of youth, and my mind wandered back to my own University days when life was a breeze and I had no cares in the world.

We all have the ability to just be. To be our true ourselves. Somehow life gets in the way and before we know it, we have been swept up in the roller coaster of society's beliefs, values, and expectations. We don't even know it at the time, it is just the path we are supposed to take. But who says you have to?

I spent twenty five years living a life that wasn't my path. I was not unhappy with that, I met my husband during that time and had two beautiful daughters, but I didn't listen to my inner voice. The voice I should have listened to and not the voices of people who didn't know my path. It took many years to change direction and live the life of my dreams.

If I could teach my children anything, it would be:
follow your own path. Your inner voice will tell you what to do,
you deserve to live an awesome life.

I love this quote from Einstein.

"Out of the clutter, find simplicity. From discord, find harmony. In the middle of difficulty, lies opportunity."

Why don't they teach that at University?

I had become all evangelistic standing there in the church, something about this place brought out the inner preacher in me, I'm not even religious. Places do that to you.

Durham Cathedral is huge and beautiful. Its Romanesque towers loom over the entrance and the façade is dotted with little windows. Inside it is even more impressive. I was pleased at the lack of crowds there too, it was late in the day (which is probably why it was quiet), but I had that magnificent building to myself... what a bonus.

That kind of thing happened to me on a few occasions. We were in Paris shortly after an International incident, and I had the Mus'ee d'Orsay to myself that day too. I got to see all those famous masters' paintings, without one person standing in front of me. I sat there for hours just gawking at those stunning works of art, like I was having my own private viewing—almost unheard of in such a famous building.

There I was again, standing in another magnificent building... alone. I closed my eyes and took a deep breath. I never tire of that feeling of wonderment, that many people have walked these passageways, halls, and walkways in history. I wish time travel did exist sometimes, just to go back for a day would blow my mind.

It was time to meet my family for dinner and I headed back to the restaurant a few minutes before our meeting time, and ordered a glass of wine.

The river was like glass, not a ripple to be seen. Little wooden boats were moored against the embankment, all lined up in rows and empty, after a day's work out up and down the river. How perfect to have dinner in that most wonderful location.

There were little restaurants and boat clubs lining the banks, brightly displaying blue and red market umbrellas which gave it a festive atmosphere (or the Union Jack, now I come to think of it).

The restaurant tables were decorated with gorgeous recycled tin teapots with bright orange gerberas poking out of the spout. The menu was extensive and covered, "Old fashioned favourites and modern British cuisine".

I have some gorgeous photos of Raymond and Coco from that night. We are all relaxed, and my children were more than happy to pose for photos this time, funny what a difference a few days make. Three days previous they were both moaning about having their photos taken, and in Durham they were all smiles. I was very happy (and my husband didn't look like Derek either). It had been a lovely evening, and as we walked back to our hotel across the river, the night was in full swing, the town numbers swelled into the thousands I expect, all enjoying the sultry springtime air

How do you make memories? I have a few ideas.

The trip was ours to discover. No matter where we chose to go on holiday, it didn't matter. In life, it's not where you go, it's who you travel with. Travel sets you free from modern life, allowing you to travel your cares away, quite literally. It is not about the past, or the future, it is about being present. You can step back in time, especially when you visit family and connect with your ancestry, but memories are made in the moment.

CHAPTER 13 – YORK

Another destination we visited back in 1998 was York. I remembered it affectionately–and we were en-route there. Built during the 13th century the city walls of York were some of the most impressive surviving mediaeval fortifications I had seen.

Inside was a fascinating array of medieval streets, Georgian town houses, modern shops, riverside pubs, and the crowning glory: the York Minster, England's largest Gothic cathedral.

There were spires for miles around. Being a compact city inside those walls made driving into the centre difficult, so we opted to use the park and ride system on the outskirts of York.

There were large car parks dotted around the fringes that house thousands of cars. Given that York can attract millions of visitors a year, we thought it best to park the Mercedes and catch public transport. It was a great system really.

We heard on BBC radio news that a storm was brewing in the neighbourhood, and it was likely the warm sultry weather would turn and we would be faced with a downpour. It certainly didn't deter us and we headed for the centre of York.

The bus dropped us pretty much in the centre of town and armed with our smart phones, we set about finding 'The Shambles'. It is an old street in York that dates back as the far as the 14th century (wow!). The shops overhang the cobbled streets and some looked like they were on such a lean I worried about walking underneath them. It was the cutest place. The Tudor style buildings had flower planters along the tops overflowing with ivy and geraniums, and a few were even festooned with coloured lights. Some had the most unusual windows I had ever seen, with tiny panes of glass all stuck together with lead light that tipped outwards to let in fresh air. Some of those windows had at least sixteen small panes in various rectangular and diamond shapes.

Along there we happened across a food market with what I can only describe as the largest meringues in the world! I think they were called 'swiss' meringues and you could feed a family of four with one, they were the size of your hand. There were more flavours of meringues than you could poke a stick at, chocolate and orange, chocolate and honeycomb, white chocolate and raspberry and mint aero. The girl's eyes widened and their mouths hung open, I knew what was coming. How could I say no to those snow-white beauties? They all looked so delicious.

We ordered four different flavours at what I thought was a reasonable price of £1 each, and took our bag of goodies to the nearest park bench. The last time I had a meringue I was a child, and there we all were, munching away with white powder spilling onto our laps, looking forward to our sugar highs. Sometimes it was the smallest things that brought me so much joy. A simple recipe of egg white and sugar could conjure up wonderful childhood memories of school fêtes, Christmas festivities, special treats and Nanna cooking in the kitchen. I was heady with whimsical memories of being a child and the magic of meringues—maybe all that sugar was affecting my brain.

We had a lot on our to-do list in York, but it was such a pleasure to just walk the streets. The centre was well sign posted with heavy green and gold markers showing the direction of many attractions, and the time it took to walk there.

York Minister was on our list, but first we took a stroll towards Kings Square and the Holy Trinity Church. Right in the middle of the road a newly married couple were having photos taken outside the church. The bride had a beautiful fish tail wedding dress with a floating veil. Being Saturday, it was a normal day for a wedding, but all the same quite unexpected.

The sheer size of York Minister took my breath away. It was enormous. The central tower alone stands at a height of 72 metres. It was amazement by the bucket load. I could have stood there for hours just looking at it. But right on cue (courtesy of our BBC weather reports), big plops of rain burst from the sky and we scurried to the front foyer to escape the imminent downpour, along with fifty or sixty others.

Our visit was a bit earlier than we expected, but given the weather conditions outside taking refuge in the magnificent church was quite comforting. As fortune would have it, we were just in time for the free guided tour.

I was buoyed by the prospect of touring the Minster with a well-informed local but the girls didn't share my enthusiasm (again). The tour was an hour and a half and according to them it was akin to being told they were about to go to prison.

"You will learn new and exciting things about this significant building," I said, trying to make it sound like they would enjoy it. When I cast my mind back to when I was a teenager, I agreed it was far from what I would have wanted to do. The word 'dreary' came to mind. Anyhow, we were there and we took our spot in the group, then proceeded on to meet our guide.

York Minster is the Cathedral of York, and was the seat of the Archbishop of York, the second highest office of the Church of England. According to the website, "Before the building you see today, there have been at least three other minsters on or near the cathedral's current site. The first known reference to the cathedral is in 627."

It was one old building. I was astounded at the history in that country, it was hard to conceive significant moments in history happened right where we were standing, it really blew my mind.

In the vastness of the nave, I was overcome by just how beautiful the building was. The intricacies of the stone work, the marble statues, the twinkling stained glass windows, the endless roof span ... my head was spinning and not just from craning it backwards to view the marvels.

I was interrupted from my stargazing by the dulcet sounds of an English gentleman, "Welcome to York Minster." Our guide was probably in his early sixties and fit exactly what I thought a guide to a church would look like: genteel, and wearing a fine gauge knit, with padded elbows and sensible shoes.

He explained he was a voluntary guide, which I thought was fabulous. He was so passionate about teaching people about his place of worship, that he went there in his own time to spend an hour and half with a bunch of strangers. You can't get any better than that.

Like the RNLI I mentioned earlier, there are thousands of organisations in the UK that rely heavily on the generosity of volunteers.

Taking a guided tour is really the best way to see and experience any attraction. We learned so much about the cathedral I cannot even remember half of it, but I will try.

One of the masterpieces of York Minster is the Great East Window, a stunning display of stained glass. It was commissioned in 1405, taking three years to complete. The window depicts the beginning and end of all things, from the creation of the world described in the book of genesis, to the events that will presage the end of the world and the second coming of Christ, as told in the visionary book of revelation. It is the size of a tennis court.

In 2008 (600 years later!), 311 stained glass panels were removed to be restored by experts at the York Glaziers Trust. They painstakingly restored half of the panels with the remainder due to be finished in 2018. There was an excellent display detailing how they went about restoring each panel. It was meticulous work, and I for one thought it was amazing those people are continuing the ancient craft.

The National Lottery funded large chunks of money towards the restoration, and it is marvellous public money was being committed so future generations would be able to enjoy those masterpieces.

Our guide was informative, funny, and engaging—even the girls got something out of it–and they were genuinely surprised how much they enjoyed it. Tick!

As we headed back outside, the rain had cleared and it had become quite steamy and humid. Most peculiar weather for England, but none-the-less I found it quite pleasant as we headed towards Dean Park.

Dotted along the pavement edges were rows of gorgeous little old fashioned caravans. They had been converted into mini cafés and the one we spied for lunch had cupcakes and ice cream and was painted a vibrant shade of pink. Wooden chairs and tables were laid out right in front of the park with the backdrop of the cathedral as the view. The grass was covered in tiny little daises and there was definitely a vibe of summer in the early afternoon. It could not have been a more perfect way to spend an afternoon.

We had all good intentions of stopping in Cambridge for the night on our way back to Sandgate, but had left our run too late for accommodation and there were only two options left. One was hideously expensive, and the other was just plain hideous. Even the surrounding areas had nothing available, and although we were disappointed we wouldn't get to visit Cambridge again, the children were keen to get back to Sandgate.

I have fond memories of Cambridge. I particularly wanted to take the girls punting, it was a fun thing to do along the Cam River and some of the sights were wonderful.

I distinctly remembered the Bridge of Sighs and Trinity College as we navigated our way up the river. Punts are similar to Venetian gondolas, only without the curviness. Punts are narrow and have flat bottoms. The punt was created in the mediaeval period to allow access to areas with shallow water, and today were used mainly for recreation or by fisherman working in marshland.

Punting looked easy, but according to my husband from our previous visit, was not. Steering a punt was not effortless, and his first few attempts landed us in the grass reeds of the river bank. I remember the scene in Bridget Jones' Diary where Hugh Grant and Renee Zellweger were rowing on their romantic mini break and they were ceremoniously dumped out of the boat into the water. It didn't happen to us, but there were a few times the pole got stuck in the mud of the river bottom.

I was keen for the four of us to experience that charming part of Cambridge, but alas we didn't have anywhere to stay so we bypassed Cambridge and headed south along the M1.

We stopped at a roadside service, which was neither outstanding nor awful, just the in-between lack of character you find in featureless nondescript groups of buildings. It only offered takeaway food options, but given I was on the hunt for caffeine, I was pleasantly surprised to have three options to choose from.

After the obligatory toilet stop, I happened across a rather large garden at the rear of the building that had chairs and tables with fancy umbrellas. There was also a large pond and a grassy mound with deck chairs. It was quite the oasis beside a busy motorway, and we decided to stay there while we mapped out our route.

From there it was nearly a five hour drive to Sandgate. A family conference was needed. We explained to the girls we could stop a bit further south of Cambridge for the night and return to Sandgate the next day, or really hot tail it and get back that night. Our ETA would be around 8pm so it would be a long day.

As we sipped our hot beverages we contemplated the Mercedes mission and came up with a plan. We phoned ahead to Jules and Kate and announced we would be back that night. They very kindly asked what we wanted for dinner and said they would wait for us to return before firing up the BBQ.

There was that twilight highlight again—at 8pm it would still be light enough for an outdoor meal. It was also a bonus for our driving program as we were going to hit the M25 ring road around London and we had no idea how busy it would be. Given our experiences early in the trip, we were dubious about the estimated time it would take and hoped we wouldn't be arriving at our friends at 1am with charred sausages on offer.

Our drive along the M1 was rather uneventful for which I was glad, no diversions, detours, or bypasses, we actually sailed down the motorway (not quite wind in our hair, but it was pleasant in a monotonous sort of way). We had to cover over 400 kilometres to get back to Sandgate so we strapped ourselves in for the long haul. It wasn't an unpleasant drive, the roads were well signed, smooth, and 120 kilometres an hour, but it was rather dull.

We were patting ourselves on the back for such a clear run on the road, when we realised it was a long weekend in the UK. Monday was a Bank holiday. Well that explained why we couldn't get accommodation in Cambridge. It had not occurred to me to check.

We have public holidays in Australia, but they were mainly limited to Easter, Christmas, and New Year. (Although we do have a day off for a horse race!) We didn't have bank holidays like they did in the UK.

It was May when we visited, and there were two bank holidays: May Day and Late May.

May Day was an ancient northern hemisphere spring festival and originated from the pagan festival of Beltan. Over the centuries it had been thought Romans celebrated the coming of spring with a day of dancing and allegiance to the goddess Flora. The maypole was also deeply entrenched in Pagan tradition. Traditionally made from birch, the maypoles were constructed by villagers as a sign of community. Maypoles were generally decorated with flowers and ribbons, and people danced around them hanging on to long ribbons.

Aurora was born in London on May Day, not only did she arrive early, the public holiday made the drive to the hospital speedier than usual. We didn't name her Flora, but she does have a traditional English name, dating back to Shakespearean times.

The Queen Elizabeth II Bridge across the river Thames at the Dartford Crossing was quite the wonder of engineering. I had never seen it before. It rises up over the Thames like a giant cable spanned sea monster.

It was a scenic drive over the top, but I had to remember to pay the toll by midnight the next day, otherwise it could be up to a £108 fine. It's pretty steep when the toll fee is only £2.50, and I was sure our friends wouldn't be impressed at receiving that bill in the mail.

Driving through Kent with the bright sun hanging in the afternoon sky, gave me time to reflect on the past week. I had enjoyed myself enormously. I didn't have a favourite part as such, I just loved spending time with my family.

They were precious moments. I re-created a holiday from nearly twenty years ago, and while some things hadn't changed, some things had, and I couldn't have been happier to share it with my children and my husband.

In 1998, I had never thought about being a parent, let alone being a parent of teenagers. I didn't have a short memory, I knew what teenage girls could be like, but that was not my experience at all. Both the girls took everything in their stride, they participated when they needed to (without too much angst), they settled into life on the road, didn't moan continuously about having their knees up to their ears in the back seat, smiled and were generous with their time when it meant something to me, and were polite and always asked for permission to buy something or go somewhere. They were generally upbeat about 'boring' tourist attractions, listened to experts about history, and feigned interest to the best of their ability. They tried new foods (except haggis—I didn't even try that one, but Raymond did), laughed and giggled like school girls (which they were) ,and soaked in their surroundings, appreciating they were so fortunate to be travelling the world. We had had the time of our lives, I was very proud of them.

CHAPTER 14 – BACK ON THE COAST

We made excellent time and arrived back in Sandgate just before 8pm. Jules and Kate were waiting with champagne bottle and glasses in hand, ready to dispense as soon as I unbuckled my seatbelt. What a welcome, we were very happy to see them.

The weather was still warm with an evening breeze blowing in off the beach. It was perfect. We had survived our driving holiday, no speeding fines or parking tickets (as far as we know), no chipped paint on the duco, no flat tyres, no driving up a one way street the wrong way, and we were all still taking to each other, so an excellent outcome. It had been a long day and we were all rather tired but happy by that stage.

It was familiar to be back in Sandgate with Jules and Kate. The girls headed upstairs to the comfort of their room and flopped on the bed, connecting into the Wi-Fi.

Raymond and I welcomed a soft sofa and a glass of wine with our friends. We recalled our last seven days with humour, exasperation, and pride. We had two days left in England before the long haul flight home and we wanted to make the most of the time we had left.

The following day was a bank holiday (the Late May one!) and we decided we would book a water front restaurant for another English tradition I love: the Sunday lunch (except it was Monday). Being a public holiday, it kind of felt the same.

The restaurant catered well for the holiday lunch crowd, and we booked a table for six near the window, overlooking Folkestone harbour. It was a modern looking building with black curved walls and glass doors. It was busy there, (I think everyone had the same idea as us), and we headed to the bar on the second floor while we waited for our table.

The view there was wonderful, albeit a bit windy, which meant we couldn't sit outside. The Folkestone Harbour was undergoing quite the facelift. That place, like many others along the coastline, had a rich history, and it is fabulous these ancient buildings were being restored for future generations. No country in the world does restoration and renewal like England, which is one of the reasons I love it there.

It was quite the grown up restaurant, especially for our children. We had spent the week eating in pubs and supermarket sandwich bars so it was a treat. There was something lovely about eating at a fancy place, we didn't do it often, but it was one of those life experiences we needed to teach our children. There were rules.

No one wants to be sitting next to a table of sulky teenagers with bad table manners, heck I didn't want to either. From quite a young age we took our children to swanky restaurants, not often but enough that they could learn the right way to behave. Learning etiquette is a life skill because you don't know when you are going to need it.

As a child, I was always told I needed to know how to conduct myself at the table, just in case the Queen came for dinner. It hasn't happened yet, but at least I know my butter knife from my steak knife. That hasn't always been the case. I remember a particularly embarrassing moment at an upmarket restaurant, when I had no idea how to get the crab meat out of the claw. The knitting needle apparatus next to my plate was the tool for the job, but I honestly thought it was to mix my cocktail.

Our children enjoy nice places just as much as we do, and they appreciate special occasions. Sitting in that glorious location with the girl's godmothers' was a time to cherish. If time could stand still for even a day, that would be my perfect scene. The people sitting around that table were the most important people in my life, and I felt truly blessed to be there.

When we arrived back to Sandgate we had to face the arduous task of packing our suitcases ready for the trip home. It sounded easy, just throw it all back in, but that didn't take into account the amount of crap we had amassed during our holiday.

I always told the girls not to pack their suitcases to 100%, and to leave room for what they bought on holiday. They took no notice and of course we got to the end of our holiday and they could not fit everything in. Sigh... it happened every time.

We ended up having to borrow a soft sided bag from our friends and added it to our luggage allowance. Thankfully we were not over the limit, it must have been leaving that straw hat in England that tipped the scales in our favour.

The morning of the day we were leaving Raymond and I thought a brisk walk was in order, given we were about to spend a day in a steel tube. The weather was sunny but cool, perfect walking conditions, and we set off towards the seafront.

There was a very handy walking track along the beach, which was fortuitous because I didn't fancy having to stagger through the stacks of pebbles on the beach. Being Australian, it was a surreal experience, being on a beach with no sand. I was used to the fine grains filling up my flip flops (not thongs!), sticking between my toes, and generally getting everywhere—including behind my eyeballs.

The absence of the fine loose particles of rock was unfamiliar, but I was starting to get used to not seeing sand as the beach profile, at least in the UK.

The word beach in and around those parts apparently means 'pebbles worn by the waves'. I can't say those pebbles were worn much, they were still quite large in size.

The English were also trailblazers when it came to the development of the beach as a fashionable leisure resort. From the mid-19th century, there were popular spa towns springing up everywhere from Scarborough to Brighton. The aristocracy were the first to embrace those towns for their recreation and health benefits.

They were originally only for the upper crust but as the progress of the railways began the middle class and working class started to frequent the seaside resorts also. The sudden influx of travellers motivated business people to build attractions, promenades, fairgrounds, and accommodation in those areas. The growth during the 50s and 60s was extremely rapid.

Beaches are still popular destinations for holidays and as we walked along the shoreline we could see families setting up camp for the day with their beach chairs, umbrellas, and portable barbecues.

There were fishing poles stuck in the sand with long reels bobbing in the sea, cast in by fishermen with (I'm sure) the anticipation of catching dinner.

Couples lay on the shale towards the top of the beach and children happily swung their colourful buckets looking for treasures (although I'm not sure what they were trying to find).

There were a few small food stalls dotted along the beach selling seafood (and pancakes!) so I supposed if they didn't catch anything on their poles or in a bucket, they could always buy it.

In the distance was the Hythe Imperial Hotel. It was a very grand looking building, visible for miles around. It had apparently stood in that spot for hundreds of years, and was now a place of luxury for travellers. It had undergone quite the transformation (there was still scaffolding there when we walked past) and would no doubt look amazing once the renovations were finished. It was a glorious looking building and I can just imagine what it must have been like a century ago with its luxurious rooms, silk tapestries, grand piano, tennis courts, and croquet lawns. It would have been amazing to step back in time to see it.

We walked back along the Royal Military Canal, which was also a lovely walk through wild grasses, vibrant purple flowers, and overhanging trees.

Those tow paths are common throughout the UK, and I personally love them. They were tranquil paths amongst busy neighbourhoods where birds, ducks, and dragonflies resided in abundance. It was magical to walk just a stone's throw from the local supermarket to find plumed paddling ducks and fluffy squirrels.

Bumblebees are by far my favourite insect, they are the best. It is a feat of engineering that they can fly—they are enormous compared to our bees in Australia, and their fluffy exteriors and bands of gold are photo worthy. I took countless photos of them on our travels. Along the tow path they flew around, humming away to their tune. It was a lovely afternoon, just soaking up the Englishness of it all.

I was going to miss not being here.

CHAPTER 15 - HOMEWARD BOUND

It was time to say goodbye to Jules and Kate and to England. We were buoyed by the surprise news they were both coming to Australia for Christmas that year. It was a wonderful way to end our holiday.

Kate had been to Australia many years before and Jules never. She had never been on a long haul flight, and she asked me for advice. I had to be honest: I had none. As previously mentioned, I had tried everything for the 'fear of flying' traveller, and unless you are prepared to knock yourself out for 28 hours, I know of no cure. But I can guarantee you will forget about it the moment you step off the aeroplane and have arrived at your dream destination. She will love Australia as much as we love England.

As we neared the end of our holiday I asked the girls,

"What was your favourite part?"
I truly wanted to know, even if they said shopping.

I was surprised to learn that shopping wasn't the answer (I had to do a double take).

Coco said, "My most favourite part was having no schedule; we could do what we wanted when we wanted."

Aurora agreed, but also said she loved the baby lambs!

I was happy they had that perspective, the point was to slow down. Sometimes we barely take a breath and become overwhelmed by the modern world.

We had taught them they could inhabit the world with the wonders not only inside them, but outside them.

We left from Heathrow Terminal 3 for our long haul trip home. It took us close to 28 hours to get back to Melbourne from London, and the flight was not for the feint hearted.

Coco dislikes flying immensely–she had never been one of those children who were excited to be on an aeroplane. She didn't even get excited about the plane food (like most children do). Days before we left she got herself into a tizz, and it didn't matter what I said, or did, or bribed her with.

I have had some truly exhausting flights with her. Holding her hand for hours on end, talking to her about why she was so frightened of flying, holding sick bags, explaining to flight attendants that, no, she didn't want anything to eat (even after fifteen hours), mopping up tears, reading stories, flicking through endless movie suggestions and walking kilometres up the aisles of an A380. I have no advice here. I have tried everything and anything, and nothing thus far has worked.

I just keep organising holidays and hoping like hell she might grow out of it... not yet.

In spite of the 28 hour ordeal on the way to England, she skipped off the aircraft like nothing happened, and was immediately in holiday mode. I had to give her ten points for that. Once she was on terra firma she was instantly back to her old self.

I read in my research before the trip that to "expect post-trip abandonment". I could sense it already. Both children were making plans in the airport lounge to catch up with friends when they returned (after they navigated their jet lag). They were keen to rush off and spend as much time with their friends as they could before it was time to go back to school. While I understood that at the age they were, their world revolved around their friends, I tried not to take it personally. I knew they very much enjoyed the trip and understood they needed to put some distance between themselves and us. They were most likely a bit sick of us.

I knew they would always cherish the time we had together, and I hope in many years to come, they will recall their memories with fondness and affection, and tell those stories to their children, like we have to them. Someday, they will thank us.

I love the UK. The small island and her riches are endless. To see it all would take longer than a week, longer than a year, longer than a lifetime. Even on this very small scale, my family and I were captivated. I had done my job, I had achieved the unachievable.

It was the trip of a lifetime.

I will now add this to my favourite travel list, and in nineteen years' time, I will recreate it again... I can't wait.

"Twenty years from now you will be more disappointed by the things that you didn't do than by the ones you did do. So throw off the bowlines. Sail away from the safe harbour. Catch the trade winds in your sails. Explore. Dream. Discover" – Mark Twain

THANK YOU

I am beyond lucky to have so many beautiful people in my life, and the ability to travel our magnificent planet. I am ever so grateful to the following people for their love and their support.

Ray, Imogen and Trinity–my everything, always.

Annemieke and Jane HJ, who are so many things to us; fairy godmothers, travel buddies, and beautiful friends. We wish you lived closer.

Big love to Michelle, our travelling buddy in 1998. It was, and still is, one of my favourite trips.

My friends and family who are always there for me and support me in my quest to be an author.

Big love to Joanne, my right hand woman, walking partner and breakfast buddy. Your enthusiasm for life is infectious.

To Michelle and her team at Accentia, here we go again! I could not do this without you.

Big love to Anna Blatman and her gorgeous painting that adorns my front cover.

To Heather for her wonderful editing. It's a long road from writing at home to a book being published and you make that road a lot smoother, thank you.

About the Author
JANE DELAHAY

Jane Delahay is a Melbourne based author
and dedicated Yogi.

Her first book 'The Leap Year' was published in 2017
and is part memoir about her own breast cancer story
and part travel journal about trekking in Tuscany.
She has the wanderlust gene and has travelled extensively
through Europe and the UK.

Jane is married, with two daughters,
one dog and
two cats.

www.janedelahay.com

Enjoy more of Jane's writing at:
www.facebook.com/janedelahay.author
www.instagram.com/janedelahay/

www.ingramcontent.com/pod-product-compliance
Lightning Source LLC
Chambersburg PA
CBHW072050290426
44110CB00014B/1621